NIDHI ZAK/ARIA EIPE

Auguries of a Minor God

First published in 2021
by Faber & Faber Ltd
Bloomsbury House
74–77 Great Russell Street
London WC1B 3DA

First published in the USA in 2021

Typeset by Hamish Ironside
Printed in the UK by TJ Books Ltd, Padstow, Cornwall

A CIP record for this book is available from the British Library

ISBN 978-0-571-36556-2

10 9 8 7 6 5 4 3 2

शम्भुस्वयम्भुहरयो हरिणेक्षणानां
येनाक्रियन्त सततं गृहकर्मदासाः ।
वाचामगोचरचरित्रविचिन्तिताय
तस्मै नमो भगवते मकरध्वजाय ॥

I bow to that supreme lord Kāma
with his makara flag ever-hoisted

by whom the three cosmic rulers
Shambhu, Svayambhu and Hari
were made eternal servants
to their doe-eyed devis

and whose astonishing achievements
beggaring description, beyond words,
anoint him with most magnificent glory

for Baba and Amma

नेति नेति नेति

nothing
without you

Contents

स्मरसि स्मर

स्तम्भन

ചുംബനം

ammachi taught me how to kiss / my small face in her hands / cheekblade whetting mine / breathing in sharp / lungfilled as if / she had just been born / and I / so close / enough to smell / giddy heat / oiled ringlets / like coconut / like matriarch / tough brown outside / tender white inside / so

later / when he put his tongue / down my throat / I gave it back / because a man / who doesn't know / how to kiss you / doesn't deserve to / touch your hair

be/cause

because nothing is like anything
        else, an approximation will always break
                down when you need it most

because nothing is as soft as a horse's muzzle
        at the curve, above quiet punctuations of hair,
                thin pointed teeth guarding tenderness

because I had just been, that morning,
        at my college graduation – *looking gorgeous*
                in that dress – where the speaker urged:

I hope you will be vulnerable
        with each other, that you will be open
                to giving and receiving vulnerability

because he touched me without asking
        saying: *you are like nothing*
                I have ever seen before

like how I am touching this horse
        feeling its likenothingelse before, us
                two silken manes, two hurt mouths

I am so gentle with you between my hands
        but tell me / strike my face / pull away
                do you not want me to

blow slow into the open black
      tunnel of flared nostril, wet
           dark animal breathing back

that's how they kiss – a passing
      stablehand spoke in my direction –
           and I believed him

                        I believed
                not / because it was true
                but / because I wanted to

Fret

Each night this ritual
animal rises from
my lungs like

        haar

from the clutch of my
chest to the dread of our
bed as a hare in this room
                watches you with body
                still unmoved: pinned
                      by beams
                                wide with light
                                like deer: doe-eyed-fawn
                                      like pretty

शोषण

formerly exotic, fruit

I pay so much for papayas here
three euro fifty for a stunted child

> *slit their stomachs deft*
> *with a surgeon's stroke*
> *seeds a caviar clutch*
> *slick like newborn spawn*
>
> *glistening summer shoal*
> *swimming hard upriver*
> *migrating for miles just to*
> *make sure they survive*

ripe and ready, brags the sticker
yet these fruit are never either

> *shades of home stifled*
> *heavy heat remember once*
> *waiting in womb warm*
> *flushed flesh so unlike this*
>
> *jaundiced fade of cornea*
> *not yellow/orange/red but*
> *riotous relentless saffron*
> *stains like an early bruise*

hand-picked, grown in the tropics
firm with a slight yield to the touch

love when you stake this
pith black centre cleave
the blighted heart watch
my shock

	splayed tissue
fall	*at your feet*
like that	*asunder*
blameless	*bursting*

nowhere close to worth it
the price that I have paid

The unquiet amygdala

Acute   borderline personality
disorder   occurs when you've been

abandoned   neglected   abused
                                   when you were
                                        a child
and you are afraid
you think everyone
is going to hurt you everybody
is going to leave   you know
                                   everybody
                                   always leaves
[an attachment pattern   in the end
     learned behaviour]

Tests show that activity in the amygdala
is heightened in people   who are prone
to this condition   to this conditional
                                   sort of love

Experiments indicate that when you
start to   walk s l o w l y
                           towards somebody
                                   who suffers

this person is   more likely to stop
              stop stop stop stopstopstopSTOP
                                        you

at a greater distance than the unafflicted
because they   tend to sense
                an   increasingly credible
                                          threat

                        borderline beautiful, my borderline brave

                swaying   silently   gyrating pain
                in the riotous firing   gyri of brain

Sleep, melancholy

When it arrived, I could not
                    sleep turned his face
                        so far from me
                            and I called out

                        I dreamed
him there in a darkened cave
        by the river of forgetting   I begged
            that calm and gentle   god would find me
                                kiss my eyes
                        closed in enchantment
                        cover me with poppies

When it came, when it changed
                us and everything
                        we lost
                        the hands of time
                        and space
                            seemed elastic
                        shrinking into vastness

I thought of you then how I would give half of my life
for you   how you live
                        where neither rays nor waves
                        touch, you
resting on blackened bark   a twilight
                                         in bloom
stitched together   from the shadows   on your wrists

But sleep, melancholy

                  you are not alone   for death is always

                                    somebody's brother

constant youth with featherlight fingers   waltzing

                              on the sea's broad back

सम्मोहन

Ode to day

Today I am going out &
my social calendar is generally something to behold

                                    It was not always like this:

there were days when my spine screamed from lying in bed too long
listening to one cinematic dirge spool on repeat like Max Richter's
On the Nature of Daylight, which someone at *Vox* proclaimed to be the saddest
                                    song in the world &

there were days when I was more horizontal than vertical
as if I were still invertebrate, I hadn't developed a backbone &
Charles Darwin's evolutionary bipedal ape-man transitional representational diagram
                                    meant nothing to me &

there were days when anxiety prowled like a tigress
immured, awe-ful, frightening & whole nights where
I did nothing except eat oversalted gone-soft nuts & listen for a sound that would
                                    indicate you had written me &

        haven't we all been there where
                one person becomes the world &
                    thinks the world of you

            haven't we pined, mist-kissed
                in our solo showers &
                    leaned over to look out

                    of the cloistered windows &
                            let down our hair
                                for you, thief

Innocent

you said you really needed coffee so we walked into the first place with display pastries in the window and while you stood there indecisive in front of the chalkboard menu I looked so carefully at the posters plugging those coconut oil espressos, ran my fingers through the hand-picked fairly traded artisan-roasted brown beans sourced direct from the farmers' co-op in Guatemala, even waved my phone over the QR code which showed a short film of José's highland farm in Huehuetenango with its gleaming cherry-red berries, and all this simply to avoid meeting the gaze of the dark flute-boned cashier with the letters I-N-N-O-C-E-N-T embedded on the gold badge on his chest a bright star blazoned across his jersey striped with the colours of Cameroon who was asking you now what you wanted, but the thing is it didn't sound like talking it sounded as if his throat was melting and so were you and me, me too.

What birds plunge through is not the intimate space

She can't believe this jag-winged majesty
really wants a piece of her

creature stealing up
                            rising like
                            a black and leafy ledge

into the honey-bearing chaos
                            of high summer.

Everyone's voice was suddenly lifted
                            . . . O, but everyone was a bird!

But it isn't a bird
                            it's a man in a bird suit
                            a song inside him, blue
                            shoulders instead of feathers.

There is a sky, teeming with winged
things, birds with fiery plumage
winging wildly across the white
                            orchards and dark-green fields
                                        on – on – and out

of sight

a stand of white pines
                            i n d i v i d u a l flames
against the masonry of black smoke

the day-blind stars
waiting with their light.

Stillness falls like a cloud.

Suddenly she puts out her wing –
the whole, full, flirtatious span of it:

blackbird, my lord,
as nothing will hurt you
I'll sing as I love.

उन्मादन

Fugue for young & fugitive

you know you have made me
                  a fool
                  for your attention
                            you   my master
                                      piece of work
                                      of art

even when I am out with friends   sky firing into   fuchsia unspeakable purple
barelybearablebeautiful   stamping horseshoeheeled boots in the cold and wind
                  singing in our mouths

                  buskers stealing   away   looks fishing for smiles winking
                            syllables   from   our throats brittle
                  whip/lash of long hair   voices   loud   with laughter

until I start to   tear   that's when   I realise
                  tear
                  d   it's you
                  r
                  o   I cry
                  p
                  tears

                                                  for & how much I miss you

to night/bits/pieces/death/distant stars

but you know how you had me made how you turned me in
                                      to a craven begging
                                      merely a mouthpiece
                                      for your disaffection

on the run
      cut loose your name tattooed   a summons as a spell
          mark made manifest
               sirens
                  loud/blue/red/blue
              howl
    the city holds my gaze
            &   every where
                your eyes

                        arrest

Self-portrait, with shyness

Maybe I am a maned wolf
lanky, tremulous legs
as if I stepped in something
knee deep and dark it makes me
look as though I can dance or
keep it all close to my torso
this is why I skitter when alarmed

Maybe I am a maned wolf
on the inside so say you were to
slit a slight incision by my breast
place an alien object in my chest
it would show up as light and pulse
for you, my heart, watch it still
thrill now when it senses you near

for the rhythm that it makes is yours
how it swells in my belly, how I sing.

A history in stone

used to be madness was considered a stone, you say, studying that Bosch painting at the Prado. When we reach the hotel again, you will look it up on artnet, consider buying it, because you are the sort of person who still invests in things that ~~you~~ appreciate. Used to be madness was when you couldn't tell where you end/I begin. When did we make ~~up~~ our ~~minds to~~ break from this asylum? Were we not committed? Madrid: aflame in a smother of summer. Outside: hot stones, people dining al/frescos splashed across the walls of this claustrophobic city. Retiro Park: properly pretentious everywhere coats of arms, regalia, red seals like the one they'll emboss on our official split apart – but that is later

today

we have not thought to speak

the word, yet, divorce stillbreathes between us, bestial baby in our bed. Wander hand-in-hand into this past with me, perhaps we won't get hit by what we didn't see coming. We were beautiful together. In the bar across the lobby, you slide in beside me restless legs all hallows apples rallying in a sea of separation. *Listen*, you begin, your voice a tautstrung pitch. I can feel the conversation about to surge, reach for the table, steady now with/draw these lines around ourselves and all we used to be, so – *dime mi amor: is it over? is it ours?* the flailing thing that yawns, that warns: *come, no/closer, love, my madness/stone, stone/hearted lover.*

मारण

Lo(e)ss

When I was still / little
I had a teacher, a monk

                    Sometimes I'd really want
                    some thing / body
                              to stay

I'd shy up to him, ask

         what to do
           with this
              desire

                    He would take my hands in his,
                    cup them as a single heart, say

                          what are you
                          trying to hold
                                on to

Loosen your grip, see
          the whole sky
          – resting –
          in your palms

      //

Now
sometimes / still

        I walk outside

palms spread, eagled
      to sky

      and
         watch
        and

            every thing that I have loved
              falls through

                my fingers
                 like silt

Filial, at the pyre of the body burned, three days after

gone
go on

pick it up
            pinch

thumb and finger   trigger suddenshockflesh
recoil   release   drop   hot   not   what

you thought it would be what did you think
it would be porous like coral pockbruised melon
in the ocean you dove for their cauliflower heads
they cut you   feet weeping palettebrushwash
curlingsmokewisp ferrous red in sunbleachedsalt
give those sharks something to smell
                                        no

for bone is fishribsharp and flinty   as a knife   no
an entire Swiss Army swivelling sixteen glinting
silversliveredtongues heated to/with/in inches of
life serpentheadready to strike
                        god

                let everything end when you die
                allatonce now
                            all at once now

A Myth of Horses

Say a horse is a myth:

as big a myth as the bigness of a foot
or the tooth of a sabre-toothed tiger
like a lion *feliform social carnivore*

like a lie
extending so far as bone
from a cornered mouth, long in the fang,
                even when closed.

                        Say a myth is a horse.

                        Say a myth is a band is a herd
                            is a harras of horse.

                        Say we harassed a horse, say
                            we whipped it, kicked it,
                                  say we broke it.

                        Say we broke a horse
                            how would we put it together
                                        again?

Say there were only ever five
                horses five of anything.

Say we set them up let them all loose thirst tearing through their throats
in a torchered desert gave them leave to find drink and right when they
came in sight
        of that glitterdark

                oasis

                        pierced a whistle like a falcon bird
        of prey hunting them down, calling them forth, commanding
                                    their return.

Say only five of them did, so we called these

    al khamsa

        the birth of all horse on earth.

                Say a horse did not need water
                for it could hit a fisted hoof
                upon any surface and draw blood
                        like constellations.

                Say a horse did not need water
                        because it had wings, say

                        a horse is a mount
                            is a fount
                                of life.

Say horses were born to run
even though they were not

say they sleep standing up
                not lying
            down

say they move towards pressure
not spurred on by pain

say they shy
away.

Say a queen made love
to a dead horse.

Say a queen was made to lay down
love with a slain stallion
stallion worth a thousand cows, under
the sign of Sirius four-eyed dog star, say
this horse flew like a bird over a kingdom
fleeing men, survived a whole year before
being welcomed, bathed, ritually slayed
by the king
of men.

Say the day that we burned the body of love
the flames wouldn't go out

Love was just a boy with a sugarcane bow
and five flower arrows

so we put him in the mouth of a weary white mare
and drowned her there, beneath the waves, where
she still waits with a doomsday womb,
breathing bloody fire.

Say a horse is not a horse but a giant

                                                            trap

        wooden war toy besieging the beach
              soldiers armed to the teeth
                  in the belly of the beast
            two spies sewn shut in its lips.

Say a horse is a gift, don't look it in the mouth,
say a horse is the rift between us, say
we flung a spear sprung a leak in its side
yet it did not bleed, say that's why
the bat-blind sooth-seer died for saying:

equo ne credite / do not trust the horse.

Say riding a horse

                for the horse

is like feeling the jaws of a pride of lion
close around the flared boat of your throat
the lecherous grasp of a human predator
grappling with your jugular
imagine

the horror! as horse
            and what if this lion could speak?

Say we would not understand him.

A is for العرب

When there appeared a poet in a family of the Arabs, the other tribes round about would gather together to that family and wish them joy of their good luck. Feasts would be got ready, the women of the tribe would join together in bands, playing upon lutes, as they were wont to do at bridals, and the men and boys would congratulate one another; for a poet was a defence to the honour of them all, a weapon to ward off insult from their good name and a means of perpetuating their glorious deeds and establishing their fame for ever.

And they used not to wish one another joy but for three things – the birth of a boy, the coming to light of a poet, and the foaling of a noble mare.

Ibn Rashiq al-Qayrawani
in *Muzhir* of Suyuti (1282 AH)

and they used not to wish each other joy but for three things: the

birth of a blessed babyblue boy, the foaling of a
beautiful broadboned mare, and the

coming to light of a promising poet,
conjuring his craft in the hallowed halls and
courts of princely benefactors, though these

days, Arabs are more likely to be
depicted as tyrants and terrorists, deprived of their
dignity in demeaning stripsearches, delineated as
dogs, detained naked under blackcloaks, blindfolds,
draped over with darkhoods at Abu Ghraib, so eager to

end their lives in the echo of jihad for the promise of
enchanting slimhipped houri in heaven, so that
even the rest of us – who should know better – tend to believe
extraordinary things about these people simply trying to
exist in a hostile world, and wasn't it an Arab, Ibrahim, who famously
extended his hospitality to the angels masquerading as messengers, who
entered his tent unasked, and didn't he bathe their hands, their feet,
encourage them to eat, offer those three strangers a bed for the night,

fetch only the finest food that he could find, slaughter his
fattest, plumppinched calf just so his guests could
feast on the tenderroast flesh, feed their brownskinnedbellies
full, for perhaps he understood what it felt like to be
foreign, to be flung far from the familiar, to live in
frequent fear for your life, for those you love, to ferry
five children across the fiercefoaming sea, to
find yourself having to choose between home and
family, to flee like fugitives until you hit another
fence, to face – unflinchingly – the unassailable
fact that from here on out, so much will be
forgotten: language, flavour, fragrance – so
fragile, this freedom you fight for; so

go now, get a house in the suburbs, white fence, white neighbours, watch them
glare at you from behind their gauzy diaphanous drapes while you wheel out the
green bin, turn up their noses as if you embody the stench that you simply carry;
get your kids ready for school, gobbling down their generic milkflake breakfasts,
gathering up your collective courage, waiting for the traffic lights to turn:
green says go, you're teaching them to chant, *red says stop, yellow*
get ready, green says go, but colour means other to you, means
green card, black list, pentahued pentagon terror levels, that's what's
going through your head later as you help them with homework, to get better
grades, try to grow them up well – because you need to teach them to be
good citizens but they are only children so it's futile – they simply don't
get it: that they are not citizen, not permanent, not resident, not anything, yet
giving up when you've got this far is not an option, even on the days when
grief drags you under like a body, sunk and heavy, not a vibrant one, not a
gentle animate thing, moving, spirited beside your own, like a river, like
grace, like your wife's face the last time you saw her, alive, radiant, the
glow of youth like rosehip, like pomegranate, like sumacscatteredfreckles,
glistening on her cheeks, in her hearthauntingeyes, what you wouldn't
give now for the glittering throat of her laughter, rolling out your rug,
genuflecting in the direction of your holy stone, calling out to the glory of your
god when all you have is her name in your mouth, perfectprayerbead on your tongue;

how you miss her now, on these days when it is so unendurably
hot and summer creeps down the insides of your arms like
handheld icecream on a woodentonguestick, and you force yourself to
head out to get some comfort food for the kids who will be only too
happy to stage a mini-mutiny if they are made to eat macaroni again, so,
heaving yourself off the sofa, you make your way across the block to that Syrian
hole in the wall, kept afloat by the old guy with the stinking sweetstalebreath –
Hamza, is that his name? – who always tells you the same bloody story: the
history of the desertdwelling Middle Eastern Bedouin Arabian
horses, how Our Prophet Muhammad released his thunderous
herd to race through the sands in search of water, after a long and arduous
haul through the desert, but after they had bolted, all at once
he called out to them to return, commanded them to pay
heed to his summons, and though all of those handsome,
headheldhigh horses, with their paperparchedthroats,
heard his call, only five turned around and came
home to their master, ever faithful, and because of this
he christened them al khamsa, meaning: the five – and sure enough
here he is, yarning on about the horses again, while you wait around as his
harrowed family members slice shawarma on the sweatflickedgrill,
heap up those filler salads, the coloured cabbage, the hundred per cent
halal kebabs lined up like sitting ducks in the flimsy, folding,
half-assed aluminium containers that can never be trusted to
hold anything, though you can't complain, as they say here, everything is
hunky-dory, your life is peachy, so there's no reason for anything to
hit you right then – but it does, it comes straight for you, right at you, like a
hundred-ton freighttrainthundering down the tunnel of your trauma, and the
heaviness of everything you've been holding in, the heartache and the sheer
hopelessness, it all gets thrown together with the mundane stuff like the
harissa and the hummus and the sadseeminglettuce, the fluorescent fuchsia
hue of pickled turnips in the fatfriedfalafel sandwich; you don't understand
how all of it combines to make you start to cry, ugly snotty tears, no – to
howl – right there, like a tantrumthrowntoddler, in the middle of the suddenly
hushfilled, hauntingly silent, wholly hellish setup; damn, pull it together man:

I'm sorry, you say, *ana āsif*, as you stumble out the door, rubbing at your eyes,
I'm okay, to the concerncreaselined strangers on the street, keeping their
inquisitive children hidden behind their hips, wondering if you might have been
injured, hurrying them along – and rightly so, who would blame them? –
it's no noble thing to stick your fingers into someone else's pie, to get
involved in something that has nothing to do with you, caught up in an
incident that is probably more trouble than it's worth, and that too with an
immigrant, who knows what kind of shady situation that entails, better to remain
ignorant of any suspicious goings-on, best to mind your own business,
isn't that what the friendly woman at the resettlement office had
indicated that first time you'd gone to see her, Maryam, Mubarak and Maha
in tow – she'd said, *people here prefer to mind their own*, and you remember
in her eyes a kind of kindness tempered with a knowing of things to come, an
intimate moment with a stranger who seemed almost compassionately complicit
in your situation, yes, you've started to call it your 'situation' too,
isn't it strange how much distance language can put between you and yourself,
I can only imagine the ordeal it's been, only
imagine what you've had to go through, your colleagues at the
institute say, but you know that even if they think they can, they can't
imagine what that's like, and you forgive them, because this is not
intentional, because they probably feel an empathy born of their
instinctive human desire to connect, to regard the pain of others as
if it were their own – these are the best kinds of people – but
in truth, our suffering is first and always
individual: our engagement with the suffering of others only an
imitation of how we would approach the indictment of the offence
in question, if it happened to ourselves; it's only when we are truly
identified with something that we can claim it for our own, anyway enough
indulgence in this pointless line of thought – Marwan has
inched over to where you are standing, staring wistfully out of the thinly
insulated window; he wants to show you something (on your
iPad which he has filched from your briefcase to entertain himself,
information freshflooding his synapses): infrared images from the
infamous Chernobyl Exclusion Zone, taken by some
intrepid photographer with a full spectrum camera –
iced-over landscapes with a spooky pink tint, but everything still

intact, the skeletal bones of buildings, the abandoned
insides of cultural centres, classrooms, gymnasiums; as
if everything were eternally frozen – suspended
in time, and in the midst of that eerie desert:
irrepressible life –
insects and elk, foxes and lynx, wolves, the new
inhabitants of this contaminated rubble
– it says in the article that human activity causes more
interference for wildlife to survive than
if they are exposed to long-term, low-level radiation –
isn't it nuts, your son says, *how nature takes over again, as
if we* (he means humans) *never even mattered* – and
it strikes you, when he says it – how he chooses to use the word *matter* – the
insignificance of a life, and you're still thinking of
it when you hear the azan and head out to pray and embrace your
imam, who tells you again like he does every time:
inna lillahi wa inna ilayhi raji'un,
it is from Him we come, and to Him
is our return; after you return from

jummah, you come home to one of your overly
jovial children bursting to tell you something:
Jehan opened the door! your youngest, Maha, preens, the
joy of ratting on her sister almost imploding her face –
*Jehan opened the door while you were gone, even
just when you had reminded us not to!* and
Jehan rolling her kohllinedeyes at the
juvenile nature of the whole thing:
just please, give me a break in her sullen teenagetone; *it was a
Jay-Ho-Vah*, Maha crows, *a
Jay-Ho-Vah coming round to tell us about
Jay-Sus*; you don't know where she gets this inclination to
jazz up the pronunciation of the words in her vocabulary beginning with
J, but you understand that it's not going away any time soon; now she's
jostling for space beside you on the sofa, wants to show you her

journal from school, the question: what do you want to be when you grow up?
jOcKEY, she'd scrawled, in careful colours; you don't think she even knows what a
jockey really does, that they shouldn't grow too tall, or how
judiciously they need to keep track of their calorific intake, it's probably
just the only occupation she's heard of where you get to ride, the only
job she knows that will keep her around horses, and though she has barely
just turned six you can already see her in the gallop, long tresses trailing like
jasmine creepers, tangled in the wind, already see her trying to
justify her chosen profession to her elegant, octogenerian
jiddah, who will shake her head in despair at the poor
judgement of this new generation – *and to think that your grandfather was a*
judge, she would say, with a sigh; now Maha slides to the floor to
join her brother who has been silently playing a game of
Jenga by himself, she pulls out a tile with a
jaunty flick of her wrist and the whole tower
jiggles perilously, still – miraculously – holds its centre, a
juddering calm passing through the
joists of its construction; you call out to
Jehan to look after her siblings while you go for a
jog, to get some exercise: you haven't moved in weeks, your legs quickly turn to
jelly, after what feels like forever you stop and lean against a lamppost, take some
jagged, ragged breaths, you go to check the time, but
just then you realise you've left your phone behind in the pocket of your
jeans, and if anything happens, an emergency, no one can reach you so you
jog all the way back home and open the door to
Jehan, standing in the hallway – flaunting a bright orange
jumpsuit that seems to be the trend among teens these days – in her
jail-like garb (*orange is the new black*, she says), regarding you with those
jadegreen eyes, the same shape and depth and colour as her mother's, your fiery
Jehan, who has fixed the others some food for school tomorrow: strawberry
jam sandwiches with peanut butter and individual pouches of
juice – made from real fruit, none of that synthetic shit and all the sugary
junk they add to the food here – you keep their lunchboxes beside their ironed
jerseys so they won't forget to take them; then Mubarak rubs his belly, says he's
jolly starving, some strange slang, so you rifle through the pantry, find some
jalapeños, a box of taco shells, some black bean tins, an unopened

jar of salsa, a ripened avocado, a hardening slab of Monterey
Jack in the fridge, and you put the kids to work, give them
jobs – grate the cheese, smash the avocado, slice the tomatoes,
juice the lemon – things work better when everyone is busy, not
just sitting around with time to think of the harrowing
journey they made not that long ago, though sometimes they still get
jittery, have bad dreams, wake up in the dead of night to
jump into bed with you, as if your existence were enough to dispel all their
jinns, all the haunting memories of a life left behind getting
jumbled up with the present, tripping up the timeline,
jamming their memories, *when was it that we came?*
January – the coldest month – *and when are the long holidays?*
June, halfway through the year – *and what comes after that?*
July, and you don't know what else, what else to tell them,
just what you're meant to say because you don't know what comes after that, this
juxtaposition of the life they used to live with the one they live now, the careful
juggling act you'd have to perform – as a child – to keep it all
jiving together in your head, to remain a single, integral being when you're
just not sure who you are anymore (or were, to begin with) – thank God for their
jabber and banter, for their continuous exclamations of wonder, for their
jubilation in little things; you would probably turn out to be a bitter,
jaded man without them, now Maryam is telling the rest of them a
joke that her new friend at school taught her, she appears to have a list of
jokes about animals, *Baba, listen, she says, do you know the ans—* Mubarak
jumps in wanting to say something, but she shushes him, asks: *what do you do if a*
jaguar is sleeping in your bed? You stroke the stubble on your chin as you watch the
joy flood her face on the cusp of delivering the punchline – how you wish you could
just freeze this moment forever – *sleep on the sofa!* – and the others roar in glee,
justifying the build-up, the theatrical pause, the delivery of the lines; *I've got one,*
Jehan says now, in a radical departure from her usual reluctance to engage with the
joshing and teasing of her younger siblings: *which day of the week is a*
jaguar's favourite? They all sit back in their chairs to consider the new
joke on offer, strange riddle-me-this, and after a couple of dud answers, the
jester gives in to their pressing pleas to know and yells *Chewsday!*, and you
join them in their raucous laughter, in that simple, open-throated song of
jubilation, which any bird flying by your home

just then could easily identify: the oddly pieced
jigsaw puzzle of a family, a feather flocking together;

keeping up with all of them is a full-time career in itself, you
keep fretting over the breakneckpace they're growing at, the
knowledge of how blinkandmiss these days are
keeps gnawing at you, and you try to hold on to them by staying close; in the
kitchen, Jehan is brewing some dubious drink:
kombucha or some other achingly artisan beverage – *it's*
kind of like
kefir – she shrugs, when you try to get her to explain; the other
kids are in a tangle on the floor watching videos on YouTube, some
kalashnikov-wielding skeleton puppet – Achmed the suicide bomber, who
keeps yelling in a high-pitched squeal – *Silence! I*
keel you! SILENCE! I
KEEL YOU! your children howl with laughter every time he blurts the word
kill in evermoredesperate tones; Maryam wanders into the
kitchen and asks if she can have a
Kinder egg, she is almost addicted to these sugarshellspheres, you tell her to
keep it to one a day and she nods graciously, her cheshirecatgrin creeping
knowingly around the corners of her mouth when she spies her sister with the
kombucha – *oooh, are you making that for Kenji?* – she taunts, then almost
keels over laughing as she narrowly misses a well-aimed
kick from Jehan's long legs, skipping out to the hall singing
Kenji and Jehan sitting in a tree
K - I - S - S - I - N - G ! and you can almost feel your daughter's
keen embarrassment, the hot flush on her face, the way she betrays nothing,
keeping her
kohlcoatedeyes trained on the temperature of the tea so as not to inadvertently
kill the good bacteria fermenting in the culture, and you feel a strange sense of
kinship in this conspiracy, so you do the
kindest thing you
know how to, in that moment – you leave her to it; head up to bed, feeling your
knees struggling against the stairs, probably because you overdid the prescribed
kilometres in training for the marathon you've decided to run, in the hope that it'll

keep you sane, give you something to focus on, though lately all it's been good for is keeping you up at night, because you have been trying to count kilometres instead of sheep, visualise yourself passing the markers:

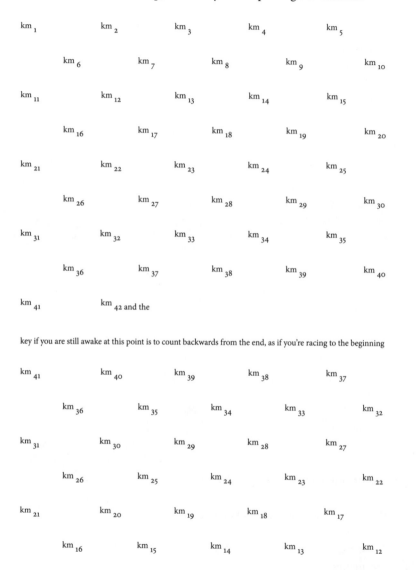

km 1   km 2   km 3   km 4   km 5

    km 6   km 7   km 8   km 9   km 10

km 11   km 12   km 13   km 14   km 15

    km 16   km 17   km 18   km 19   km 20

km 21   km 22   km 23   km 24   km 25

    km 26   km 27   km 28   km 29   km 30

km 31   km 32   km 33   km 34   km 35

    km 36   km 37   km 38   km 39   km 40

km 41   km 42 and the

key if you are still awake at this point is to count backwards from the end, as if you're racing to the beginning

km 41   km 40   km 39   km 38   km 37

    km 36   km 35   km 34   km 33   km 32

km 31   km 30   km 29   km 28   km 27

    km 26   km 25   km 24   km 23   km 22

km 21   km 20   km 19   km 18   km 17

    km 16   km 15   km 14   km 13   km 12

km $_{11}$ km $_{10}$ km $_9$ km $_8$ km $_7$

     km $_6$ km $_5$ km $_4$ km $_3$ km $_2$

km $_1$ who are you

      kidding? the

      key is to dream: *kiss

     *kiss

        *kiss

               *kiss

      *kiss   *kiss

*kiss

       *kiss

         *kiss

      *kiss   *kiss

   *kiss

     *kiss

          *kiss

       *kiss   *kiss

    *kiss

*kiss   *kiss   *kiss

     *kiss   *kiss

         *kiss

listen

     you are already starting to forget how to

look at the world   in a way that makes it stay

      waves

lapping the shore foamy

50

lines
    leaving glossy
        lips as wisps of
        lapislazuliblue
            like how this unearthly
light moves across the water how your eyes fill with it without warning, you
look down at the children's book
            lying in your
lap, the one you have been reading to Maha each night, the one where the
little rabbit
      learns that it is
          love
            that finally makes you real:

'What is REAL?' asked the Rabbit one day when they were
lying side by side near the nursery fender, before Nana came to tidy the room.
    'Does it mean having things that buzz inside you and a stick-out handle?'
    'Real isn't how you are made. It's a thing that happens to you. When a child
loves you for a
long,
    long
        time, not just to play with, but REALLY
loves you,
    then you become Real.'

            'Does it hurt?' asked the Rabbit.

    'Sometimes,' said the Skin Horse, for he was always truthful.
    'When you are Real you don't mind being hurt.'

    'Does it happen all at once,
    like being wound up,' he asked, 'or bit by bit?'

    'It doesn't happen all at once,' said the Skin Horse. 'You become. It takes a
long time.
    That's why it doesn't happen often to people who break easily, or have

sharp edges, or who have to be carefully kept. Generally, by the time
you are Real, most of your hair has been
loved off, and your eyes drop out and you get
loose in the joints and very shabby. But these things don't matter at all, because once
you are Real
you can't be ugly,
except to people who don't understand.'

love that makes you visible
love that makes you whole
love that will fill these gaping
lacunae in your bones, the hollows that have started to haunt you

lately as you have been thinking more and more about what it is
like to

lose you have started to compose
a
list
a
little
litany of
loss

like how people tend to
lose
socks or
house keys, the number of the plumber,

lists they had made out somewhere for the store,
car keys and headphones and coins and notes,
lego pieces, receipts for things that should be exchanged, glasses and
lipbalm, that elastic tracksuit bottom which is the only one that really fits anymore

lose scarves, gloves – both or more
likely just the one – hats

lose their trolleys in the brightly
lit fluorescent aisles of those obscenely
large supermarkets, the ones that won't
let you forget how much you detest these artificially
lit facilities, how they
leave you   feeling
like you never want to be
left
languishing in their bowels again

lose wallets, coloured plastic cards; not even counting the many kinds of universal
losses:

loss of teeth, for instance,

baby / milk / wisdom / rotten

like how Maha was on the verge of
losing one of her
lowerleftmolars (she had been worrying (it) end-
lessly, tonguing the ridged underside at a
lateral angle out of her gum; you recognise the
long-festering desire to be rid of it, to
let it go, the want was driving her wild)

little
losses:
those displaced, misplaced
things that are not really
lost because they can be found again
and then
literal
losses, the
losses of other things so
large   they turn all the
language in your mouth into a bilious stream of

like the reek of the carelesslydumpedcarcasses of those
lions abandoned in Baghdad

like the howl of a dying dog in the dark

like when you pass a dustkissed makeshift altar on a
long, deserted stretch of highway, its unassuming coordinates

l
o
n
g
i
l a t i t u d e
u
d
e

looking only vaguely sacred, zip-tied to a
        lamppost:
                limpdeadballoons, fadedpartystreamers, the
laminated photo of someone else's child, reflective surface catching the
last of the
        light; a carefully
                laid bouquet of
                longstemmedflowers shuddering in the seismic wave of
                                        lorries thundering by

like how you have

lost track of whether Samir is still alive, if he ever made it off
Lesvos, if he made it to shore   face up and upright, face
lean with onlydaysold stubble, not swollen and waterlogged
like a puffer fish, *please God, not*

like that –

lost track of days, months,

     track of time, its slimy black guts

lurking heavy in your hands

lost ancestral olive orchards
                appetites

lost words
       whole words, no, entire
languages even so
       like how in your dreams you are mute
       like when you open your mouth inside that
       lost, blurred world
              left in
              limbo
                        gasping for air
       like a dumbsheenfish, no different from when you wake
later, no one needs to tell you that all the world is
                lost to you now you have

lost your mind
       head
       breath

          temper
          patience
          memories

lost sleep

        your religion

lost life, breathing

living people, not just those you
liked but even the ones you
loathed, the ones you couldn't stand you
                                        wished them dead
lo, now they were   and that could
                                        likely be on you

lost laughter, the many-belled ring of her laughter

lose, now:
            love
                your love – she
                            who?

left you with only salt:
                        ocean
                            tears, a cruel trick just the

                                        lick of the sea sting in your wounds
like a foreign body
like a thing that should not be
                            here or there or
                                        left behind
like you were
            left behind

like you are now, a
lone, lone wolf, foreignbodiedwolf, gaunt and grey,
lingering at the school gate and one of the kids' friends' mothers, a carefully dressed
lady, says – *I have not met your wife yet, how is she, is she working?* and you feel
like someone has thrown you into an iron cage facing an injured,
livid, half-starved predator – the
lower half of your limbs and jaw start to tremble, you feel
lightheaded, you want to

limp into the

left half of her body, say: hold me; want to tell her: she's dead, that's how; want to

leave, and never go back, and just

like that you recall a joke that Jehan told at the table

last night: *What does the*

lion say to his family before they

leave the den to go hunting?

let us prey

let us pray:

la ilaha illallah

la ilaha illallah

la ilaha illallah, and now, after Salat al-

Maghrib; in the

makeshift

majlis in the hall,

Mubarak, Maryam and

Maha are

monkeying about,

mimicking what seems to be a

miniature solar system – not

made particularly to scale – holding

mature, fecund fruits

masquerading as planets: the

mighty sun a large navel orange;

Mars a pregnant peach,

Mercury a small, shrivelled apricot and the

moon a pockmarked bruise of striated honeydew

melon – they orbit one another's bodies,

moving around each other like

magnets, turning this way and that; the

moonmelon held in

Maryam's hands takes you back to
memories of the
muezzin calling out from the
masjid silhouetted against the first light of
muddy dawn; Hajj
                    Makka
                              Medina, remember how your children
marvelled at the
magic of the cannon firing to
mark the end of the fast during Ramadan, the
march of the
military parade down the Corniche, the crescent
moon emerging from behind a cloud; now

Marwan barges into the room, looking frantic,
madly trying to complete an assignment, a
mini-biography scrapbook project on Eadweard
Muybridge, a pioneer in the photography of
motion; he's having trouble with
multiple spellings of the
man's name and when you look up the history to try and
map it out for him, you realise it's an issue that
merits considerable confusion: he was born Edward James
Muggeridge in England in 1830, he changed his name
many times, starting with 'Muggridge', still later he
made it into
'Muygridge', and again when he
moved to America in 1867, he used the name
'Muybridge', a version he seemed content to keep for
most of the rest of his life, though the name on the gravestone is
marked – allegedly – as Eadweard
'Maybridge';

Marwan has lifted the information for his project
maybe almost entirely from Wikipedia
meticulously copying it out as captions underneath the

many photographs and illustrations that he has
mixed together to
make a sort of
mosaic of the
man's life, like:

Muybridge used
multiple cameras to capture separate
movements which the human eye could not distinguish

Muybridge was tried for the
murder of his wife's lover, one
Major Harry Larkyns

Muybridge discovered that Larkyns
might have fathered his wife's seven-
month-old son Florado Helios
Muybridge

Muybridge went in search of
Major Larkyns and upon finding him,
Muybridge said, 'Good evening,
Major, my name is
Muybridge and here's the answer to the letter you sent
my wife', shooting him point-blank

Muybridge insisted his actions were deliberate and pre-
meditated, but he was finally acquitted on the testimony of
multiple witnesses that a severe head injury had
markedly affected his personality and state of
mind

Mr Leland Stanford, Governor of California, hired
Muybridge to settle a bet he had
made, using pictures of one of his
mares, Sallie Gardner

Muybridge perfected the
method of photographing horses in
motion

Muybridge was influenced by the stop-
motion studies of Étienne-Jules
Marey, a French photographer known for
major groundbreaking work in producing
multiple-exposure, sequential images using his
Marey wheel camera

Muybridge made a sequence of
multiple images of the San Francisco
Mint during the period 1870–72

Muybridge's pioneering work in
moving images inspired
Marcel Duchamp's 1912 painting, a
modernist classic and one of the
most famous of its time

maybe all of this extensive information about this
man – which seems so superfluous now –
might be useful to him some day, though it's
more likely that it will turn out to be
meaningless trivia that simply
multiplies in his brain until it is forced to
make way for new experiences, newer
memories; he seems
more or less finished with the
main bulk of his
mission, so you leave him to
mind his own and go to check on the girls – they all sleep in the same room now

much the same as you do with the boys, there's a new poster
marking territory on the door (until now there had only been one, a row of spotlit

milk bottles and the words COME IN WITH THE
    MILK COME IN WITH THE MILK COME IN WITH THE
    MILK COME IN WITH THE MILK COME IN WITH THE
    MILK, repeated over and over): an arresting image of a
man you recognise as Behrouz Boochani – Jehan had
mentioned him – an asylum seeker, journalist, Iranian-Kurd, who
managed to escape from Iran, but was intercepted on a boat crossing from
Malaysia or Indonesia and later detained in the
Manus Island Detention Centre for years; he composed his entire
memoir through text
messages written in Persian and translated by a friend, tapped out on his
mobile phone: *No Friend But the*
Mountains, the poster reads, *Writings from*
Manus Prison, a book that had won a
major award recently, you can't remember which,
Maha is already in bed, she wonders if you wouldn't
mind telling her a story before she sleeps; she loves
most the ones that have to do with
mystics and prophets so you tell her again, about
Mūsa, and how he parted the sea, a
miracle that she always
mimes with raised arms and a
magnificent smile on her face:
magic, Baba, she says, that trademark spark of
mischief in her eyes, *if I pray enough*
maybe one day I can
make the sea
move too? and your heart
melts and you tell her
maybe you can, that if she has just as
much faith as can fit in the
miniature heart of a
mustard seed, she can

              move

                    mountains; now when you
move to the door to turn out the light

Maryam calls to you from the other bed –

Monday night is her friend's fancy dress party and she has
made up her mind to go as somebody called
Maleficent, *she's a Disney*
movie villain, Baba, she
mutters, sighing audibly,
making exaggerated expressions with her eyes,
more than a little unimpressed with having to instruct you in this
matter, showing you pictures of a woman with horns like a
mountain goat bandaged with black
masking tape on her head – *I need some*
make-up so I can do the red lips like
Mama used to; the kids so rarely talk about their
mother but when they do it's so casual, almost
maddening: as if she were still alive, still in the
midst of everything, as if she would
manifest, walk in the door, any
moment now, you can't make out whether their
memories fade at a faster rate than yours or if it's even
more simple: that the impulse to
mourn does not linger in their
minds, as it does in yours, and they have
made their peace with her passing, refusing to
magnify their loss any
more than necessary – you
mull this over as you drift into a
muddled sleep, stretched on the sofa (as if it
matters, there's no one waiting for you in your bed anyway, no one
missing you or wishing you would bank your warm
musk next to their own), and you sleep in fits and starts like a
manic
       marionette, waking with hypnic jerks to a past that is no
more part of your reality, a persistent pattern until you wake for real and go through the
motions of your new life, lecturing on
migration studies and

marking academic papers and you can't believe it's been
more than a year now since you all
moved, since
meaning shifted like the ground when it
moved – withoutwarning – beneath your feet, and how this has
marked you and how you will not know how
much until

      much

          much later –

                  maybe all of this weighing heavy on your
mind is the reason why you are unreasonably tired when you finally
make it home, having had to
make an unscheduled stop at the school for a parent–teacher
meeting with
Miss Jennings –
Mubarak's
maths teacher – she specifically called you in, it wasn't just a general term
meeting and you wonder what he
might have done, he's not usually one to get in trouble, you think as you sit on a
makeshift bench borrowed from some kindergarten classroom and watch her
manicured fingernails
moving through the air, waving about as if they were trying to conjure something
magical from their
          mildmanneredtips, she was telling you:
Mubarak doesn't show
much interest in playing sports
most of the
morning break he spends reading, he has such a sharp
mind, such a formidable
memory, I would really encourage you to put him in the advanced
mathematics class next year, he could also join the junior
MENSA club, they meet every
Monday . . . your mathematically inclined son, where did he get that from, you
muse – definitely not from your genetic
make-up – and then, out of nowhere, another

memory: how his first words were *Allah hu Akbar*, he heard them every day from the
mosque overlooking his bedroom window, your shy
middle child with his camellonglashes, but you can't tell
Miss Jennings that, even though she seems like she
might be sympathetic, even though she
most likely wouldn't take it the wrong way, still – you're not
mad enough to risk it – and besides, what difference would it
make to her, to anyone else, this
memory which is yours alone now – *the other day he came up to
me and said
Miss, please, caress me if I'm wrong*, and her eyes
misted over, though she blinked them quickly to
mask her tenderness, and you wonder why she felt the need to
make herself seem tough in the face of the sentiment she felt in his hearthushing
mistake, as you pause now by the mailbox to bring in the
mail, ill-equipped for the
mayhem that awaits you soon after you have flung your heavy coat on top of the
mess of jackets by the door, sunk into the softstomachedsofa, inadvertently
made a little steeple with your hands and pressed it to your forehead, when something
makes the fire alarm go off and it's screaming sonic

murder at a

mad frequency:
Maha is running in circles around the hall, her hands
muffling her ears like one of those three wise

monkeys,

mystic Japanese

macaques,

Mizaru – or was it the other one: Kikazaru? – saying *oh
mygodoh
mygodoh
mygod, oh
my god, Baba,
make it stop, can you
MAKE IT STOP*, you find
Marwan in the kitchen,
momentarily deafened, wrestling with the unnecessarily complicated

mechanism to open the windows,
mouthing his apologies to you over the banshee wails, you finally
manage to unscrew the deafeningwhitedisc and the ensuing silence is almost
magical, everyone blinking like newborns in the
mercy of the quiet, *sorry*, your son
mumbles, as you watch him shake out the
mangled smoky black triangle into a
mess on the counter, *I was just trying to*
make the khubz crispy so I put it in the toaster; you tell him to
make sure to check the settings before he puts such a thin slice in,
Maryam dispensing some pop culture advice as she
mills about, wagging her finger:
Marwan, you've got to check yourself before you wreck yourself; some part of you
marvels at how effortlessly she has
managed to pick up this slang, this accent while another part

                                          mourns for the loss of her
                         mother   tongue, for how language
mutes itself, how it goes
                  missing; atrophies and rusts –

maybe home is in your
mouth, in the words, those
mornings when you catch sight of yourself in the
mirror, and don't recognise what you see, it's only when you
move your
        mouth to speak that you hear the
                      music which still emerges,
music that these days everybody seems to hear only in their own heads, through
massive headphones, like Jehan who has returned from her
morning workout with her headphones jammed around her cranium, not
mindful of how loudly she is singing the lyrics to a song –
maybe you just walked away
        man, walked a-way from your
                mind, I think you know, how this
                      might go – oh-oh, and the words

make you stop, dead in your tracks, you feel like she
might as well be singing about you,
maybe you're that
                    man
maybe you've walked away from your
        – meanwhile, one of the kids has called your wife's
mother to report the incident; she still thinks it's
miraculous that you can talk to your family on the other side of the world for free,
Marwan dispensing the impressive trivia he has gathered through copious reading: the
most expensive spice in the world is vanilla, particularly
Madagascar vanilla, which is actually from
Mexico and pollinated by a rare black
Mexican bee, and that the
most expensive tea is called *bai*
mou hou which
means white
monkey tea and grows on the side of the Taimu
mountains in China and is called that because the leaves are covered in
many-fingered longlightwhite hair that
makes them look like the paws of those
monkeys, and did you know that the
most expensive coffee is civet coffee, which is named after the Asian civet cat called
musang which eats the coveted cherry fruit, then poos out the bean, which is what
makes it taste so unique and irresistible – a fact which sends
Maha into a fit of giggles; when they pass you the phone, you have so little to say, her
mellifluous voice so like your wife's you almost can't stand to hear it, you tell her
Maryam attempted her recipe for Umm Ali, that birds
– magpies,
            mostly – have started coming to the garden,
Mashallah! she says, and
means it, you tell her you are happy; what you do not tell her is how you
miss her daughter, how you wish you could just see her – for a tiny
measure of time, no – for a thousand
                                million
                                        measures of time, but not this time, this
moment, not even in your dreams – for it is, again, another

morning; you turn on the news and something is breaking, all over the
media – *our correspondent is at the scene bringing you the latest on this*
morning's massacre at a
mosque in the city of Christchurch in New Zealand: a
man entered the
mosque while
Muslim worshippers prayed – and
murdered them, en
masse, it was being called the country's worst
mass shooting,
multiple deaths, at least forty or
more, now
more details emerging – that it was being considered a terrorist attack, the accused: a
man thought to be a white supremacist, he had written a seventy-four-page
manifesto which appeared to be based on anti-immigrant
motives, protesting against the growing wave of
migrants and spread of
multiculturalism in Europe, it was unclear whether the
marksman was acting alone, though he seemed to be the
mastermind behind the operation, he had carried out his
malicious attack using easily
modified semi-automatic weapons – known as a civilian's
machine gun – they were investigating the
make and model of the guns he used, though it was believed he
must have acquired them legally, targeting
migrants, the attack was livestreamed on social
media, *Facebook now scrambling to take down any copies of the*
material though their AI algorithms cannot keep up and
multiple anonymous websites are now host to the
massacre at the Al Noor
mosque . . .
        but you cannot bear to listen any
more because someone else has breathed her
                          name

                                    Noor
Noor
            Noor
                  Noor   her
                  name resounds in your ears; you

need to sit down
need to catch your breath, stop your head spinning, stop the world spinning out,
now a protest rally is passing, marching, a moving mob, a bodyofblur shifting
near the window – young people striking for climate action, chanting
not in our name, your own daughter is part of it though you want to tell her
no, somehow you still pretend as though everything is
normal even as you want to grab her, shake her shoulders, tell her how it is
not safe here anymore

                              no

        not safe any

                  where anymore

            no more

                  no more   no no   no more
                  no more   no more
                                          no more   never again   no
                        no more   no more   no more
nonononono no   no more   no more no more
          never again   no more   no more no more no more
                  no more   no   no   no
                  no more   no more no more   no more   no more no
no more no more   no   no more   no more   no
never again   no more   no more   no more   no
        no more   no more   no more   no more no more   no
no more never again
                        no more   no more   no more   no more
        no more
        no more
no more   no more   no more
                  no more   no no more   no more   no more
            no more no   never again
            no   no no more   no more   no more
    no no more   no more   no more
                        no more
no more   no moremore never again
        no more   no moremore
        no no no   no more   no more   no more   no more
                                    no more no more

no more
no more   no   no more no nononono   no more
no more   never again no more   no more
no more   no more   no more   no   no   no more   never again   no more
no more   no more   no more

never again   no more   no more no more no more
no more   no more   no   no no more   no   no
no more   no more   no   no more   no no more
never again more no more   no more   no more   no more   no
no more   no more   no no no   no more   no more
no more   no more   no more   no more
no more   no more no   no   no no   never again no more
no   no more   no   no more   no more   no more   no more
no more   no more   no
                                    no no   no more   no more
no more   no more   no   no   no more
no   no   no   no more   no more   no more
no more no more   no more   no more   never again
no more no more   no more   no more   no more
no more no more no no more more   no more   no more
no   no   no more no more no more no more no more
no more   no more   no more no more   no mor never again
no no no   no more   no more   no no more   nonononono
no no more no more no more no more   no no   no more no
no more no more no more   no more   no more   no more
no more
no more   no more   no more   no no more
no more   no more   never again no more   no more
no more   nonononononono
no more   no more   no more   no more   no no
no more no more no   no no no more no no mor   no no more
no more no more no more more no more   no more no no no no no
no more no more   no more   no more no more   no more
no more no more   no more no more no more no no more no more
no more no more no more no more no more no more no more no
no no more   no more   no   nonono   no more
no more   no more   no more no no no no more more no more no no
no more no more no more no more no more no more   more no no
no more no nevenonogain no more   no more no no no more   no
no more no more no no no more no no more   no no more no more
nono no more no more no no more no no more no no more no more
no more   no mano more   no more nononononononono more no more
no more no more no no no more no more no more no no no more
no more no more no more   no mo no no no more   no more no no
no more no more no more   no no more no more no more no
no more no more no more no more no more no more no more
                                    no

no more

never again, no.

69

O you who believe! Face the difficulties
of life with patience and perseverance. Eat
of the produce of the earth that is pure and lawful.
O people! If you wish to worship God, eat
only of the pure things provided for your sustenance.
O you who possess knowledge and wisdom! The law
of fair retribution is a source
of life: by adhering to it you may be restrained from desiring the death
of those who murder and instead be content with compensation.
O you who believe! Fasting is a duty prescribed to you: you must carry
out this duty in all circumstances until you die.
O Prophet! There are some whose descriptions
of the reality
of belief and fear
of God will amaze and astound you.
O you who believe! Aspire to the peace and harmony that is Islam;
O you who believe! Do not render futile your charity – be it
obligatory or voluntary – by reminding others
of your largesse,
or by hurtful allusions
or scathing words.
O you who believe! Spend in His cause
of good things you have earned and the fruits We have produced

for you in your gardens and

orchards. And do not aim at
obtaining tainted goods in
order to give them away as charity; if you were to receive such goods you would be
offended. Know that God does not need your charity: He is free
of all needs and worthy of all praise.
O you who believe: fear God's wrath!
O you who believe! When you enter into a transaction that involves future
obligations in a fixed period of time, record it in writing.
Our Prophet believes in the Quran which has been revealed to him.

O people of the Book! Why do you reject the signs
of God to which you yourselves bear witness? Come and follow the religion

of Abraham. His way was a way
of moderation, a middle way. He
obeyed none but God and worshipped him and no
other. It was Abraham, who constructed the *ka'ba*, the first house
of the people. Abraham built the *ka'ba* in the crowded valley
of Makka: exalted and eternal, a centre
of guidance for all beings. In that valley the clear Signs
of God are evident: one such Sign is the Station
of Abraham, the place where he stood to build the *ka'ba*, laying stone
on stone to a height of nine cubits. Say:
'O people of the Book! Why do you reject the Signs
of God, when God is Witness to all that you do?' Say:
'O Jews and Christians! Why do you keep the believers from God's path in
order to protect your
own authority and safeguard your own position?'
O you who believe! Fear God as he ought to be feared and be ever in a state of
obedience and submission. Be on your guard lest death seek you
out while you are in a state of recalcitrance and rebellion.
O you who believe! You were the best of men to emerge from your society in
order to reform it. You enjoin upon the people what is good, and forbid what is bad.
O you who believe! Take only your fellow believers as your friends.
O you who believe! Do not attempt to fight against God. Fear God's wrath.
Obey God and His Prophet so that you may enter into His Mercy.
O you who believe! If you listen to, and
obey, the unbelievers they will force you to go back,

if you turn back it will be your loss.

O you who believe! Do not be like those who, when their brothers die abroad
or are slain in battle, reject the will
of God and say: 'If
our brothers had not left
our sides they would not have died
or been slaughtered.' Thus does God reveal the mystery of the pre-ordainment
of death and murder so that the hearts
of those that flee the battlefield might be filled with sorrow and remorse.

Indeed if you die,

or are slain, His Forgiveness and Mercy in the Hereafter
are greater than the transient glory
of victory in this world. They are far better than any amount of wealth
or fame that the lovers
of the world are able to amass. If you die,
or are slain, your end will be the same: you shall all be gathered together before God.

O people! Fear the wrath
of your Lord, Who created you from a single soul;
O people! Fear the wrath
of God in Whose Name you swear your
oaths and conclude your contracts with others.
O people! The sanctity of the ties that bind you – be they ties
of common humanity
or ties of kinship – necessitates your compliance with
Our commands, even if you do not believe.
O you who believe! Do not pray when you are drunk, be it from sleep
or wine. Wait until the intoxication has passed.
Whatever good comes to you is from the
One who put the laws of nature at your disposal,
whatever evil comes to you is from your
own selves as a result of your misuse of those laws. We sent you to preach
Our Message so that they might learn these things
and put them into practice. Whoever
obeys the Prophet has in reality obeyed God, for the commands of the Prophet
of God are the commands of God Himself. And whoever rejects the commands
of the Prophet has in reality rejected the commands
of God, not the commands
of His Prophet. No Prophet has been sent to force people
onto God's path: all men are free to bow willingly to his commands.
On the basis of principles
(of law and judgement) used by those in former times, do not defend any
one who is ready to betray his
own soul, thus setting a trend for traitors to be acquitted.
O you who believe! In obeying the laws
of God, be strong and just, and in acting as His witness stand firmly

on the side
of fairness and impartiality, even if it be to the detriment
of yourselves, your parents, your children
or your children's children.
O you who believe! Believe in God, in His Messenger, in the Quran.
Obey God and His Messenger and the laws enshrined in the Holy Book.
O people! The Prophet has come to you in Truth from your Lord, so believe in him.
O people of the Book! In following your religion, do not go to extremes,
do not say anything
of God but the Truth. Jesus Christ, son
of Mary was simply a prophet
of God, he was God's Word that took shape as a man, in the womb
of the Virgin Mary; he was of the spirit
of the Lord . . . the Lord, your God is
One God, not two or three. He is Exalted above the ascription to Him
of sons. Whatever exists in the heavens and
on earth belongs to Him, and He is Sufficient as a Disposer
of the affairs of the cosmos and the creatures within it.
O people! There can be no doubt that God has sent you irrefragable proofs
(of the veracity of His Message), for We have sent down to you the light
of Truth itself.

O you who believe! Honour all agreements you enter into.
O you who believe! Show respect for the Symbols
of God and do not violate their sanctity, nor that
of the Sacred Month, nor
of the animals brought to the *ka'ba* to be sacrificed. Help
one another to do good and to attain a state
of God-fearing righteousness; do not help
one another in wrongdoing and transgression. Most
of all fear the wrath
of God, for His punishment is terrifying in its severity.
O believer! Forbidden to you are dead meat, blood products, the flesh
of swine, and the flesh
of any animal that has not been slaughtered in the Name
of God. Also forbidden to you is the flesh

of those animals killed by strangulation,

or by the blow from a stick

or a stone,

or by a fall,

or by being gored by another animal,

or being attacked by a predator and dragged off to be eaten. In all

of these cases the animal becomes classed as carrion and is thus unlawful to you.

O you who believe! Whenever you prepare to pray, wash your faces and y-

our hands and your arms to the elbows. Then pass your wet hands

over your feet as far as your ankles. If you are in a state

of ritual impurity (following the emission

of semen), perform the greater ablution by washing your whole body

(or immersing it completely in water).

O you who believe! Keep God's laws and bear witness with justice and equity.

O you who believe! Recall the bounty

of safety and security that God bestowed

on you when a group

(of unbelievers) plotted to take you unawares and do you harm.

O people of the Book! Now

Our Prophet has come to you in

order to make you aware of your misdeeds, and to uncover for the people much

of that which was revealed, but which you used to hide from men's eyes and ears; most

of your wrongdoings He will pass over in silence.

O people of the Book! Now, after a break

of some five hundred years during which the world was without a Divine messenger,

Our Prophet has come to you in

order to show you your faults and set you

on the Straight Path; lest you say: 'No prophet has come to give us glad tidings

(of the Truth)

or to warn us

of God's wrath!' And so

Our Prophet comes to you now, bearing glad tidings

(of God's Mercy) and warning all men

of the Day of Judgement. Indeed, God has power

over all things. Remember the day when Moses said to his people:

'O my people! Bear in mind the bounty God has bestowed

on you by appointing prophets from among you,

and by making you kings and leaders
of men. Bear this in mind, for He has given you things

which He has not given to the people
of any other nation.
O my people! You are to enter the Holy Land, for God decreed that it be yours.'

The people
of Moses said:
'O Moses! The people who live in this land
of which you speak are
obstinate and unruly; moreover their power exceeds
ours, and we shall never be able to enter that land unless they (are forced to)

leave it first.
Only when they have left will we be able to settle there.
O Moses! While that land is in the hands
of such wild intransigents, we shall never be able to enter.' Moses said:
'O Lord! I have power only
over my brother and myself; these people have gone astray and no longer
obey me.' God said: 'I forbid them to enter this land: for forty years it will be
out of their reach, during which time they will wander through the wilderness.'

O you who believe! Do not fall into sin. Theft is a crime and the thief – male
or female – must be brought to justice. To punish the thief, you are to cut
off his or her hands to the wrist; in this way you may make an example
of them, thus deterring
others from committing the same crime. But if,
once he has committed the crime, the thief repents and puts right the wrong,

returning to the
owner the things he has stolen, then God will accept his repentance.
O you who believe! If any of you turn away and reject the faith,

the loss will not be God's.
O you who believe! Do not take as friends and protectors

those who ridicule your religion.
O Prophet! The Islamic community will need a leader and protector to watch
over them
once you have departed this earthly life, just as Jews and Christians stood in need

of new leaders
once their prophets had died.
O you who believe! Alcohol and gambling – especially the Arab practice
of casting lots by means
of arrows – are evil and the works
of Satan. Shun them, so that you may be free
of their pernicious effects. Accept
Our counsel and
obey God and His Prophet; keep to the Straight Path and beware
of Satan and his machinations.
O you who believe! When in *ihram* garb do not kill game,
                              even if the animal has been caught
outside the Sacred Precinct by a person
or persons not wearing *ihram* robes. If a believer does so intentionally,
                              he must sacrifice
one domestic animal and bring it to the *ka'ba*;
                    the animal must be equivalent in weight, value
or nature to the
one he has killed, as determined by two just believers among you.
O you who believe! Do not ask
out of turn or at unsuitable moments about matters which,
                         if they were explained fully, would
only bring you trouble. In this way, you will not be accused of meddling in things not
of your concern and thus branded an unbeliever. God is not the author
of pagan superstitions such as those
of the *bahira*, denoting a female animal that has given birth five times;
or the *sa'iba*, an animal that has given birth ten times;
or the *wasila*, an animal that has given birth to five sets of twins;
or the *hami*, a stallion that has sired ten offspring. God has not decreed that the ears
of animals thus designated must be slit, their meat declared unlawful.
                                        This is a superstition.
O you who believe! Guard your souls (from evil).
O you who believe! When
one of your number is about to die, his will must be made in the presence
of two just and believing men; if you are
on a journey and death approaches while you are far from the community

of (Muslim) believers, you may take two Jews
or Christians as witnesses to your last will and testament.
O you who believe! Fear God and listen well to His counsel; and do not dis-
obey him, for He does not guide those who are disobedient and rebellious.
One Day God will gather together all
of His prophets and He will ask them: 'What reply did your people give to you?'

And the pr-
ophets will reply: 'If the people had belief in their hearts, we were unaware
of it:
only You have full knowledge
of those things which are hidden.'

O people! The
One Who nurtures and sustains you is God Almighty. He draws the veil of night
over the face of day and makes light cover darkness

so that day and night follow each
other in quick succession. Your Lord has created the sun, the moon and the stars, all
of which
obey His command. May He be blessed, for He is the Nurturer and Sustainer
of all worlds! When you petition your Lord, expressing your needs, call
on Him – the Creator
of the sun, the moon and the stars – humbly and in private: do not cry
or shout, for God does not love those who
overstep the bounds of propriety.

O people! Your Lord is God, Who created the heavens and the earth in the space
of six days and established Himself on His Throne
of Power, administering and governing the cosmos in accordance with His Will.

He is the
One who nurtures and sustains you, He is your Lord. Worship Him and take no
other God as your object of veneration, except Him, Lord
of the heavens and the earth. Why will you not take heed?

'O my Lord! Make this land
one of safety and security and preserve me and my
offspring from the worship of idols!

O Lord! These stone effigies have led many astray;

if Your guidance is not forthcoming, the
offspring of my son, Ismail, will lose their way: whoever follows me is
of me, even though unrelated by blood; whoever rejects my mission is not
of me, even though he be my son.
O Lord! I have placed
one of my two
offspring in this parched and barren valley in the shadow of Your sacred House

in order,

O Lord, that my progeny may establish regular prayers.
O Lord! You know all that we try to hide, and all that we
openly reveal: in the heavens and
on earth there is nothing that can remain concealed from God.
O Lord! Make me one who
offers regular prayers. And,
O Lord, accept this prayer and answer it accordingly.
O Lord!
On the Day of Judgement, encompass me, my parents and all
of those who believe with Your Forgiveness!'

On that Day the righteous will be in the Gardens where rivers flow.

O people! Is the One Who creates all things like the
one who creates nothing? All things which exist in the heavens and
on earth, be they ordinary living beings
or angels, bow down before God in
obedience and humility. For they all fear their Lord Who is watching them from
on high, and they all do as they are commanded. God has made your homes places
of rest and repose.
Out of the skins
of animals He has given you tents to dwell in: when you are
on the move, they are easy to carry, easy to pitch. And from the hair and fur
of your animals, He has given you garments and
other fine articles
of luxury to serve you, and trees to protect you when the heat is
oppressive; He has provided you with caves and

other places of shelter to protect you from the cold and rain.

God showers these bounties
on you so that you may give thanks to Him. Do not coin similitudes for God, saying:
'Our God is like a great landowner with vast estates who parcels
out land to his tenants and sets
overseers to look after his concerns'; or 'God is like the
owner of a treasury who leaves the running
of the business to his accountants'; or 'God is like a sultan

who leaves the administration
of his empire to his ministers.' Say nothing
of the kind, for only God knows (Himself): you do not.

On that Day, a group of young men took refuge in a cave, saying:
'O Lord! Grant us mercy and show us a sure way to escape this maelstrom
of affliction.' The cave was situated slightly north
of the Tropic of Cancer and faced south-west. Standing in front
of the cave, you would have seen the sun to your right. And as it set, the rays
of the sun would shine momentarily into the cave, gently touching the backs and sides
of the sleepers. This cave, with its extraordinary location and ambience, is
one of the Signs of God, given in
order to guide the just. And if you had looked at their eyes,

you would have seen they were
open, even though they were deep in sleep. Their dog lay sleeping at the entrance
of the cave, its paws
outstretched. So too did we awaken them in
order that they might question
one another.
One of them said: 'How many hours have we spent here?' Some
of them, noticing the position
of the sun, said: 'So exhausted were we that we slept for a whole day!'
Others said: 'Maybe we have been asleep for
only part of a day.' Eventually they all agreed, saying: 'The Lord knows best whether all
of us have slept for a whole day
or only part of a day. Now send
one of your company into the town with this silver coin.

He is to find the market stall – the

one that sells the choicest food and buy some for you. He must tell no
one of your existence. For if the people become aware
of your existence they will either stone you to death
or force you to accept their faith, in which case you will never achieve redemption.'
One of the group, a young shepherd, went down
into the town with the thousand-year-
old silver coin; thus did We make the people
of that time aware of the existence
of the Brethren
of the Cave and their longevity. When this tale is rec-
ounted, a (new) controversy will soon emerge. Some will say: 'There were three
of them, and the shepherd's dog was the fourth.'
Others will say: There were five of them, and the dog was the sixth.' Another group
of people will say: 'There were seven
of them, and their dog was the eighth.' Say: 'My Lord knows better than any
one else their exact number:
of all the people,
only a few are aware
of how many were there in that cave.' So do not argue amongst yourselves
over the number
(of sleepers) unless your discussion
(of the matter) be in the
open. In this way, if those who
oppose you speak from ignorance, there will be
others to reprimand them. When you are debating an issue, do not ask any
one to reveal his opinion
(on the affair), for if he should give the correct number
(of Brethren) you would have to confirm it,
and thus acknowledge his wisdom needlessly. S-
ome say that the Brethren stayed in the cave for three hundred and nine years.
Say: 'The Lord
of the cosmos knows best the number
of years they stayed in the cave. All that is manifest
or hidden in the heavens and
on earth is known clearly to him. He is All-Seeing, All-Hearing. No
one but God is Master of mankind; He alone is their Helper and Protector,' the

One Who Created the earth and raised the heavens high above it.

Have you heard the story
of Moses? Moses and his wife were lost in the desert near Mount Sinai.

Catching sight
of a fire some way
off, Moses said: 'Stay here and do not move; maybe I can bring back a torch to light
our way; maybe, if there is someone tending the fire, I can ask directions

so that we may find
our way
out of the desert.' When Moses reached the fire, a voice rang out:
'O Moses! It is I, the Lord your God! Take
off your shoes for you are now in the sacred valley of Tuwa. Tell Me,

what are you holding
on to in your hand? Moses looked at his staff and said:

'It is my staff: whenever tiredness
overcomes me I lay my forehead against it and sleep standing up.' His Lord said:
'O Moses! Throw your staff to the ground!' Moses threw down his staff whereup-
on it changed into a writhing serpent. Moses took to his heels in fright. His Lord said:
'O Moses! Pick up the staff and do not be afraid; I will return it to its
original state and it will serve as a miracle to confirm your prophethood. Now place,
O Moses, your right hand under your (left) armpit and take it
out again: when it emerges, it will be white and shining. This is not a sign
of serious illness
or anaemia; rather, this too is a miracle sent to confirm your status as My Apostle, as
Our Prophet, and these two Signs have been sent as evidence
of the truth
of your mission and prepare you for an even greater sign.

Indeed, We bestowed favours
on you
once before, We spoke to your mother in her dream, saying: "Wrap your newb-
orn child in swaddling clothes and place him in a wooden casket, then toss the casket
out into the Nile; it will be the task of the Nile to throw the casket
onto the riverbank, there to be found by
one who is both My enemy and the enemy
of the child." And so Pharaoh found you and accepted you as his
own; but I cast a mantle of love

over you from Myself. And your sister ran along the riverbank never letting the casket
out of her sight until she was sure that you were safe in the arms
of Pharaoh's courtiers. Then she came to the palace gates, and when Pharaoh's
officers set
out to look for a wet-nurse, she said to them:
"Officers! Shall I acquaint you with a good wet-nurse who will look
over and care for your child as you wish?" And so We returned you
once again to your mother's loving arms, so that her eyes might be filled with light
once more at the sight
of your beauty, and her grief might come to an end. The rest of your story, you know
only too well.'

'O my people!' Noah said, 'Worship God for there is no
other God than He.' The leaders
of the people, who rejected Noah's mission, said to their followers: 'This man is
only a human being like us. The bearing
of God's Message is surely a mission
of the angels: if God wills, He shall send an angel. We have not heard
of a prophet being sent by God during the time
of our forefathers! Thus he must be mad
or suffering from delusion: treat him gently for a while
or until his condition improves.' After years
of preaching and despair, Noah called
on God, saying:
'O my Lord! Please help me for these people accuse me
of lying.' And We instructed Noah, saying: 'Build an ark in
Our sight and with
Our guidance and inspiration. Then, when the waters
of the earth begin to rise, take a pair – male and female –
of each species
of domesticated animal and put them
on board, together with your
offspring and their families. Do not attempt to intercede
on behalf of the wrongdoers, for they must all drown. And when you have embarked
on the ark, say to your fellow travellers: Praise be to God
                                        Who has saved us from the evils

of those whose hearts are black with sin.' Say:
'O Lord! Let our ship come to rest at a place where blessings and bounties

are abundant!
Only You are able to lower the level of the waters and allow us to disembark.

In this story
Our Signs are manifest. And after the people
of Noah, We created another generation and We sent a Messenger to them, saying:
'O people! Worship God for there is no
other God but He.' The leaders
of the unbelievers among them who had rejected the idea
of a Hereafter, and upon whom We had bestowed many bounties and blessings, said:
'O people! This man is not an angel. Like you he is a man. If you
obey a human being, your loss will indeed be great.

Does he promise that when you die
or your body turns to dust, you will then come to life
once more and be raised up from your graves? There is no life apart from the life
of this world: this earthly existence is all we have. Some
of us are dead, some alive. But we shall never come back to life
once we have died! This man is nothing but a liar.' Saleh said to his Lord:
'O Lord! Help me against these people who call me a liar!' His Lord said:
'One morning in the near future they will wake full
of remorse.' And after the Thamud We brought
other communities into existence. We sent
Our prophets to those communities
one after the
other: whenever a prophet appeared with God's message, the people would call him an
outright liar. So We destroyed them all and joined them with their predecessors. And
of their fate We made a story to be told. Then We sent Moses and his brother,

Aaron, with
Our Signs and a clear proof
of the Truth. They accused Moses and Aaron
of falsehood, but in the end they were destroyed. And afterwards We sent many of
our prophets to them: the son
of Mary and his mother were among
Our Signs. To each of
Our Prophets We said:

'O messenger! Eat
only that which is clean and pure, and perform righteous deeds.

I have perfect knowledge
of all that you do. The path to which I have guided you is the path
of leadership, that confirms you in brotherhood. And it is a path which you must pass
on to those believers who come after you, in
order that the community may persist in strength and unity. I am the
One God, your Nurturer and Sustainer: fear Me and no
other.' But the generations of believers who came after did not uphold the unity
of the prophets: each community went its
own way and the brotherhood
of believers, and
of Islam, splintered into countless sects and groups and parties, each rejoicing in its
own narrow doctrines. So leave them to wander in ignorance for a while.
On no soul do We place a burden
(of responsibility) greater than it can possibly bear. In
Our Presence there is a Tablet which tells the truth
of what each person says and does, and whether his deeds are accepted
or not; although such a record exists, no
one's rights will be transgressed against.

No, the people have not the slightest knowledge
of this hidden Tablet
or the criteria according to which it functions. The hearts
of the people are covered in ignorance. And there are
other deeds which they do that are not in accordance with the criteria
of this Tablet: nevertheless they continue, in the hope
of some reward. He Who is God the True Master – He is exalted above the possibility
of having created something for fun
or in vain. There is no god but He, Lord
of the Throne
of Honour. Whoever invokes, besides God,
other gods
or idols with no proof
(of their divinity) will be dealt with by his Lord. Say:
'O Lord! Forgive me and bestow Your Mercy upon me, for You are the Most Merciful
of all those who show mercy.'

84

O people! We have sent down a Book so clear in its Message that any failure
on your part to adhere to its teachings will bring upon you the curses
of future generations. Many were the nations and communities
that We destroyed in the past
on account of their sins; and when We had destroyed them, We put
others in their place. Whenever they sensed
Our approach (to punish them) they would flee from their places
of refuge. Do not flee! Return to your warm beds! Return to your houses,
or your gardens,
or your palaces. Return, that you may settle your accounts. But
on that Day, they will say:
'Our sorry fate is sealed, for we have committed acts
of evil.' We have not created in vain the heavens
or the earth and all that exists between them. Had We wished to busy
Ourselves with some idle pastime, We would have created some trifle from the realm
of the unseen and busied
Ourselves with that – if it had been
Our will to do such a thing. In broaching the subject
of what God wills
or does not will, We do not wish to philosophise. We explain these things in
order to hit falsehood
on the head with the rock
of reason and logic – to hit it so hard that its skull cracks
open and its brain is smashed to pieces. Woe betide you people
on account
of the superstitions you weave for yourselves! Whoever
or whatever exists in the heavens and
on earth belongs to Him. If there existed in the heavens and upon earth
other gods beside Him, the cosmos would be thrown into chaos.
Glory be to God, Lord
of the Throne of Power; He is Exalted.

O mankind! Fear your Lord, for the convulsion
of the earth at the time
of the Resurrection will be an awesome, terrifying thing!
On that day, the earth's continents and land masses will be floating in space.

O mankind! If you have any doubts about the Resurrection, consider how you y-
ourselves were created in the first place. We began your creation out
of pure dust, which then developed into a sperm, which We placed in the uterus
of the female and joined it (with the egg); gradually it took
on the form of a leech, clinging to the wall
of the womb. We nurtured it until it took
on the appearance
of half-chewed meat. At this stage, some foetuses continue to develop, while
others, imperfectly formed, are either aborted
or are later born malformed. We explain these points
                                            so that the creation and development
of the child in the womb may become clearer,
                              and that you may bear in mind that the aborted
or miscarried foetus is a human being nonetheless.
                                    Then We deliver you and bring you
out of the womb as a fully formed newborn baby. Then We entrust you to the care
of your mother and father, so that you may grow,
                                    mature and fulfil your potential. Some
of you die in infancy, some in youth, some in
old age. Whenever a man dies, his seed is taken by the angels
                                            while his body decomposes
over time and returns to the soil whence it came. Some
of you reach extreme
old age and grow senile; after knowing much you then know nothing.
                                                Such is the cycle
of human life, a path which man might tread hundreds
of times. Your Resurrection
on the Day of Judgement is merely the culmination
of this natural cycle, and your second creation in the life to come will be similar to y-
our first. It will differ in that you will appear not from the womb
of your mother but from the bowels
of the earth. If you consider this to be impossible, you
only need to see how the earth is barren and lifeless; then rain falls
out of the heavens and the earth comes to life, producing all kinds
of beautiful plants and flowers in pairs. This revivification
or re-creation God puts before you so that you may grasp the fact that He is the

One Truth, the sole Reality. He creates nothing in vain; nor,
once He has created a thing, does He leave it to its
own devices. It is He Who gives life to the dead so that they may see

the results and fruits
of their trial
on earth. And it is He Who has absolute power
over all things. Know that the Hour
(of extinction) will come. About this there can be absolutely no doubt.

And know that
on that day, God will raise up all
of the dead from their graves. There can be no doubt that God will admit all
of those who believe and do good works to Gardens
of Heaven through which streams
of peaceful water flow. Such is God's promise to man for the Hereafter. H-
owever, God makes no such promise
(of felicity) to man in his worldly life, lest he wait for bounties to fall into his lap,

then renege
on his belief in God when those bounties fail to appear. God indeed carries
out what He wills; and He will help the believers in times of trouble and hardship. No
one is to complain
or feel bitter about the life that God has decreed and determined for him. Instead,
one should cultivate trust in God and hope in His Mercy. If any
one is angry
or dissatisfied with his lot and imagines that God will never change his situation
or help him in this world
or the next, then let him climb a ladder into the heavens and, by way
of a short cut (to supposed felicity and better days), let him take up residence in some
other world. Then let him consider whether the solution he has
opted for is able to eradicate his problems and bring him happiness! Your God is
One and His command is
one also. So
obey His command and humbly submit your wills to His. And convey the good news
(of Our Message) to those who submit their wills to His in humility and sincerity.
Our Lord is God the Compassionate. God is the Nurturer and Sustainer
of mankind, not an enemy
out to deprive him

of all opportunities. He is the
One Who merges the darkness
of night into the light
of day, and the light
of day into the darkness
of night, so that man may be tested. Indeed it is God Who hears the prayers
of His bondsmen and sees all that they do. This is because God is the sole reality: all
of the gods and idols they call
on besides Him are false, mere figments
of their imagination. And God is Great, Most High. God is the
One Whose knowledge encompasses all things, however subtle
or profound, for He is aware
of every aspect
of His creation. Do you not realise that God has perfect knowledge
of everything that exists in the heavens and upon earth? For there is a record
of everything He creates, preserved
on a pre-eternal Tablet in His Presence: such a thing is easy for God.

O you who believe! Bow down in prayer and prostrate yourselves before
Our Lord! And try to perform the very best
of deeds, so that you may attain salvation.

O you who believe! Do not enter houses
other than your
own until you have asked permission
of and greeted those in them. If you find that no
one in the house returns your greeting, do not enter
on your own, wait until they are ready to receive you formally. If there is no
one at home,
or if you are asked to go back, go back at
once and postpone your visit until another time. It ensures that no allegations
of impropriety are made against you. And God has complete knowledge
of all that you do. God is the Light
of the heavens and the earth. His Light may be symbolised by this:

                                                       imagine, in a recess, an

oil lamp; the light

of this lamp is encased in a crystal glass which shines forth like a brilliant star,

lit by (the

oil of) the blessed
olive tree. This is not an eastern
olive tree, which receives
only the rays
of the morning sun, nor is it the western kind, which receives
only the rays
of the western sun. The
oil in the lamp is so pure that it appears luminous even before it is lit.

Here indeed is light up-

on light! And God the Compassionate guides whomsoever He pleases to His light.
O you who believe! Do you not see that all beings that exist in the heavens and
on earth praise their Lord constantly? Do you not see the birds
of the air which fly in formation like arrows, migrating to
other climes? Each being knows its
own mode of glorifying God, and praying to God. And God has complete knowledge
of all that they do. The kingdom
of the heaven and the earth belongs to God, and all beings shall return to Him.
O believer! It is God Who changes day to night and night to day, in the alternation
of darkness and light there is a sign to lead those with understanding and vision
onto the path of Truth. God creates each living thing from water,

some creatures creep

or crawl
on their bellies; some walk upright
on two legs,
others on four. God creates whatever He wishes, for He has absolute power
over all things. Those who
obey God and His Prophet, who fear God and do what is right and good – they are the
ones who will attain the ultimate victory of Paradise.
Obey God and obey the Prophet! If you
obey him, you will be guided (to the Truth); if you do not
obey, the Prophet will not force you. Know that whatever exists in the heavens
or upon earth belongs to God. He knows what you do

and what you intend in your hearts.

Our God has absolute knowledge

of all things.

One day, Moses entered the city in disguise so as not to be recognised.
On approaching, he saw two men fighting, apparently to the death:
one of them was a follower of his, the
other an enemy, The follower, nearing defeat, asked Moses to
offer his aid. Moses struck the Copt with his fist and killed him. 'Such violence
on my part is surely inspired by Satan, for he is an enemy who misleads man
openly,' Moses said to himself, and so he prayed, saying,
'O Lord! I have wronged my
own soul and thus put paid to any hopes I might have had
of liberating my people.
O Lord, please forgive me!' And so his Lord forgave him, indeed the Lord
of Moses is Forgiving and Most Merciful. Moses said:
'O Lord! To show my gratitude for this bounty You have bestowed
on me, never again will I help those who do wrong.'
                                        Fearing he would be apprehended, M-
oses roamed the streets in anguish, pondering his fate.
Once again, the same man who,
only the day before, had enlisted his aid against the Copt, approached in
order to ask his help again. As Moses lunged forward to hit the man,
                                                the man said to him:
'O Moses! Are you going to do to me what you did to that
other man yesterday? Truly you are bent
on violence and tyranny! You have no intention whatsoever
of being
one who commands peace and puts things to right!' At this point, there came
one more man, running as fast as he could, from the
other side of the city. He said:
'O Moses! The Egyptian senate is in session and the decision is being taken
                                                to execute you f-
or the crime you have committed. You must leave this city at
once; I tell you this
only because I want what is best for you.' Fearing for his life, Moses left the city.
                                                He prayed:

'O Lord, save me from the clutches

90

of these evil creatures!' All praise belongs to God, Who

originated the creation
of the heavens and the earth. It is He Who sends the angels with His Message, some
of them fly with two wings, some with three,
others with four. The Lord
of the heavens and the earth adds to His angels' wings as He pleases:
Our God's creative act is continuous, and He has absolute power
over all things. When God
opens the gates
of mercy to man, no
one can prevent him from entering, when God withholds his bounties from man, no
one can grant them in His place. For He is the Almighty, Full of Wisdom.
O people! Bring to mind the countless bounties that God has bestowed
on you. Is there a creator,
other than God, who is able to give you sustenance from the heavens
or the earth? It is God Who has created you from a speck
of dust: the speck
of dust He transformed into a sperm, and from the sperm (and its marriage to the
ovum) He made you in pairs. No female conceives
or gives birth without His knowledge; similarly no
one is granted long life,
or is cut down in his prime, unless it is so
ordained in His (pre-eternal) decree. And all
of this is very easy for God. Nor are the two waters alike:
one – the water
of the rivers – is sweet and clear, the
other – the water
of the seas – is murky and full
of salt. Yet from each
of them you extract fish and
other kinds of seafood, the flesh
of which is tender and tasty. You extract pearls and coral with which
ornaments you adorn yourselves, and you watch the great ships
out ploughing the waves, seeking the bounties
of the Lord. He has made the sun and the moon subject to His Laws, each following its

own orbit
over an allotted length of time. Such is God, your Lord, Nurturer and Sustainer
of all worlds. The dominion
of all things belongs to Him, and no
one in existence can tell you the Truth
of the matter like the
One who has perfect knowledge
of all things.
O people! You need God; He does not need you. He is Free
of all needs, Worthy
of all praise. If He wished, He could
obliterate you all and create a new race
of beings to populate the earth.

O people! We have not taught
Our Prophet poetry; nor is it fitting for him to speak in verse. Poetry blossoms
only with the development
of the imagination and the emotions, while life moves forward
only thanks to wisdom and vision. The Quran is not a work
of romantic poetry: it is a reminder
of Divine wisdom and vision. It is a Book that man must read,
a Book that illuminates Truth.

One of the Signs of God is the creation
of the heavens and the earth, and the (creation
of the) animate beings that populate them. Another
of God's signs is the sailing
of ships, tall as mountains, on the
ocean waves. In the motion and direction
of the winds there are Signs
of His dominicality for those who remain patient and steadfast in the face
of difficulties at sea, and who show gratitude for the bounty
of the oceans. You must realise that God's bounties are not given for the sake
of man's self-indulgence in this transient earthly life;
treat the bounties you acquire as goods
of this world, given merely to sustain you during your sojourn

on earth. God speaks to no man directly; indeed, man is inherently incapable
of receiving Divine speech. God speaks to His bondsmen through inspiration,
or from behind a veil,
or by means of angelic messengers who reveal whatever He wishes. And thus by
Our command We inspired you with the revelation
of God's message. Before this you had no idea what the revelation was,
or what belief in the Quran entailed, but We made the Quran

a lamp with which to guide
Our bondsmen, those whom We wish to guide; and you too shall guide men
on to the Straight Path with the light
of the Quran – the Path of God, to Whom belongs all that exists in the heavens and
on earth. Know that all affairs are ultimately referred to Him; the end
of all things is in His hands.

O people! We sent this Book down during a blessed Night in
order to warn mankind.
On that Night, every act requiring wisdom was made separate from the
others – by a command from
Our Presence. For it was according to
Our will that We sent Mercy from the Presence
of your Lord. Your Lord hears and knows all things: He hears the prayers
of the people and is aware of their inner and
outer states. He is the Lord
of the heavens and the earth and all that exists between them. If you are men
of conviction, then you will understand. There is no god but He.

O you who believe! If you help (the cause
of) God, He will help you in return and secure your position
on the field
of battle. This is because God in His Compassion is the Supporter and Protector
of those who believe in Him. With-
out a doubt, God in His Compassion will admit those
of you who believe and do good works into Gardens beneath which rivers flow: rivers
of water, ever clear and never stagnant; rivers
of milk, ever fresh and wholesome to the taste; rivers
of wine, a constant delight to those who drink from them; and rivers

of honey, pure and refined. For those who fear God there is every kind
of fruit in abundance – and forgiveness from their Lord.

O you who believe! In speaking and voicing your
opinion, do not put yourselves before God and His Prophet.
O you who believe! Do not raise your voices above the voice
of the Prophet. In equating
obedience to the Prophet with
obedience to Him, God reveals His absolute knowledge and wisdom.
O you who believe! Do not let men
of one tribe
(or community) mock
or ridicule the men
of another: it may be that the belief
of the latter is stronger than that
of the former. And do not let the women
of one tribe mock
or ridicule the women of another: it may be that the belief
of the latter is stronger than that
of the former. Do not malign others
or call them by
offensive and humiliating names.
Once a person has come to believe, he
ought to realise that to speak ill
of others – be it through defamation
or the use of
offensive nicknames – is a sin; those who persist in this sin,
                           which is a legacy from the age
of ignorance, will be counted among the
oppressors, those black
of heart and deed.
O mankind! We have created you all from
one man and
one woman, and We have made you, through-
out the centuries, into families and tribes so that you might come to know
                                 your place and p-

osition in the human race. Your heritage may prompt you to enquire into the history
of different cultures, the science
of genetics and the study
of racial characteristics, the handing down
of knowledge and the growth
of various civilisations – but it should not lead to pride and bigotry.

                                                    Nothing is a source
of pride and honour, unless God has deemed it so.

On the surface
of the globe there are
(obvious) Signs for those who possess certainty. In your
own souls too there are Signs; do you not
open your eyes to see? By the Lord
of the heavens and
of the earth, these words are true – as true as the fact that you think and speak,
one with another. Has the story
of Abraham's respected guests reached your ears?
On that day, they approached him saying, 'Peace be with y-
ou!' And Abraham replied: 'Peace be with y-
ou!', then said to himself: 'These are strangers to my home.'

                                            And so Abraham went int-
o the kitchen, and from there to the inner apartment
of his house, where he informed his wife and instructed her to take care
of the guests. Then he brought a fatted calf to the guest chamber and placed the tray
of food down before them. The guests would not come forward to eat

                                                    and so Abraham
offered again, placing the tray nearer to them, saying, 'Will y-
ou not eat?' But the guests still would not eat, and thus Abraham felt a sense
of danger. His guests said, 'Do not be afraid, for we are angels.'

                                            And they informed him
of the good news that he would soon be father to a wise, knowing son.

                                                Abraham's wife wh-
o was attending to them anxiously, came forward and,

                                        striking her cheek with the palm
of her hand, uttered a cry: 'How can

one who is barren produce a child?' The angels said:

'The Lord has decreed in this very state
of old age and barrenness you and your husband shall conceive a child.

Your Lord is All-Kn-

owing, All-Wise.'

O believer! Does man not know that it is
only God Who gives joy and sadness, laughter and tears?
Or that it is He Who gives life and takes life?
Or that it is He Who creates all (animate) beings in pairs, male and female,

from a drop

of sperm and a fertilised egg adhering to the wall
of a womb? Does man not understand that it is
only God Who will create that seed anew and clothe it in human form a second time?
Or that it is He Who gives wealth in accordance with man's needs
or in excess of them?
Or that it is He Who cherishes and nurtures Sirius, a star in distant space?

O God Most Compassionate! He is the
One Who has taught the Quran. The sun and moon follow
orbits so precise that
one can tell with ease where they will be at any given time. The stars when they set
or the trees when they fall – all prostrate themselves in
obedience to Him. That which was light, He raised up to the Heavens;

He spread the earth

out under the feet
of man, and adorned it with fruit trees and palms, their dates hanging
overhead in sheathed bunches. And grains enclosed in skin,

with herbs and sweet basil.

O jinns and men! Which
of your Lord's works would you deny? He created man from a lump
of clay – which made a sound when struck, as though it were pottery. Thus which
of your Lord's works would you deny? He is the Lord
of the east and the west
of Mars and the east and the west
of the earth. Thus which

of your Lord's works would you deny? He joined together the salty water
                                                              with the sweet: at
one point they meet together but do not mix,
                              for between them He has placed an invisible
obstruction which prevents
one from
overcoming the
other. Thus which
of your Lord's works would you deny? From these two bodies
of water, whose lower levels commingle, pearls and coral are extracted. Thus which
of your Lord's works would you deny? Whatever exists
on earth will perish – and all that will remain is the face
of your Lord, the Possessor
of majesty and honour. Thus which
of your Lord's works would you deny? Whatever exists in the heavens
or upon earth stretches
out its hands to Him in poverty and impotence. His function is not
only to administer to the needs
of those who have nothing; rather, at every moment, He creates all things anew.
                                                              Thus which
of your Lord's works would you deny? May the name
of the Lord be blessed eternally, He is the Possessor
of majesty and honour.

On the day when the star
of piercing brightness falls, nothing will prevent it and no
one will be able to deny its appearance. It will dislodge the north pole,
                                          bringing it down l-
ower and the south pole, bringing it higher, until the two stand parallel.
On the day when the earth will be convulsed,
                              and the mountains crumbled and flung far
out into space, and the dust scattered through the heavens, whatever is in the heavens
or upon earth will declare the glory
of God. For God is Almighty, All-Wise. The dominion
of the heavens and
of the earth belongs to Him: He gives life and takes life, and He has absolute power

over all things. He is the First and the Last; He is the
Outward and the Inward: He has absolute knowledge
of all things. It is He who created the heavens and the earth in six days,

                                                      spreading His wings

(of authority)
over the heights of Saturn. He has absolute knowledge
of everything that enters the earth
or emerges from it,
of everything that descends from the sky
or rises up towards it: wherever you may be, He is with you. The dominion
of the heavens and the earth belongs to Him: the affairs
of all creation are referred without exception to God. He merges the blackness
of night into the heart
of day, and the brightness
of day into the heart
of night, and He has complete knowledge
of the secrets
of men's hearts. You must believe in God and His Prophet and spend
of the wealth He has bestowed upon you as inheritance from
others. For those of you who believe and spend
of your wealth for the sake
of God, a great reward has been prepared.

One day soon, you will all die, and all that exists in the heavens and
on earth will be inherited by God.
On the day when the poles shift and stand parallel,
one to the other, and the right half
of the earth becomes hidden in perpetual darkness,

                                                      you will see men and women running ab-
out in the dark. From their foreheads, a light will shine – the light
of belief – like a beacon to guide them. And when they turn towards the place
of flight, the light from their foreheads will go before them,

                                                      illuminating the ground underf-
oot, searching for the safest, surest passage as they wing their way forward, hastening
on to Heaven. The good news you will receive from God
on that dark Day is the good news

of Heaven: Gardens beneath which rivers flow, where you shall abide eternally.
O people! Know that the life
of this world is but a game and an amusement; the goods
of this world are but
ornaments with which people adorn themselves and their lives, a cause
of boastfulness and self-aggrandisement; and in your ceaseless pursuit
of more wealth, children and worldly companions,

you are engaged in constant rivalry with
one another. The life
of this world is like the flowers which bloom after a light fall
of rain: so swiftly do they blossom and grow. But your enjoyment
of these flowers is short-lived, for in almost no time at all the blooms begin to yell-
ow and fade; then they wither and die. You too,
once this life is through, will be transported to another world, the world yet to come.

O you who believe! God is the
One besides whom there is no
other god. He knows both the seen and the unseen. He is the Compassionate
One, the Merciful. He is the
One besides whom there is no
other god. He is Sovereign, the Holy; the Source and Giver
of peace and belief; the Guardian, the Almighty; the Irresistible, the
One Who is above all creation. He is God the Creator, the Bestower
of bodies and forms: the most beautiful Names belong to Him. Whatever exists
on earth and in the heavens declares His glory: He is the Almighty, the All-Wise.

O you who are wrapped in your night robes! Stand at prayer through-
out the night, leaving
only a little for rest and sleep. Stand for half
of the night,
or a little less –
or a little more; and whenever you rise, recite the Quran in your prayers in sl-
ow and measured tones. Soon We will reveal to you a Message,
one that is pregnant with meaning. Truly he who rises at night has accomplished
one of the most difficult tasks, and is thus in a position to receive the soundest
of messages. By the fig and by the

olive; by the mount
on whose slopes these two fruits grow; by this land
of peace and security, I swear that We created man in the very best
of moulds. We revealed the Quran

on the Night
of Power. Do you know which night is the Night
of Power? The Night
of Power is more excellent than thirty thousand nights!
On the Night
of Power, the angels and the Holy Spirit descend, bearing His commands,
                                                        and until the break

of day the angels utter but
one word: 'Peace!'

Say: 'My God is One; The cosmos is a manifestation
of His eternal Names, for He is mirrored in all things in a most subtle manner,
                                                        and He is free

of all wants and needs. He does not beget
or produce anything; and there is nothing in the whole
of the cosmos that can be likened to Him.'

Say: 'I seek refuge with the Lord, Nurturer and Sustainer
of the dawn, from the evil
of the wicked when they spread their poison; from the evil
of those who practise the black arts, casting spells and blowing
on knots; and from the evil
of the envious ones, and from their envy.'

Say: 'I seek refuge with the Lord, Nurturer and Sustainer
of mankind, King and Master
of mankind, God
of mankind'; God, besides Whom there is no
other god, is Living, the Guardian of all beings – your God is

                                One; there is no god but He.

In Memoriam

Abdelfattah Qasem

Abdukadir Elmi

Ahmed Gamal Abdel Ghany

Ali Elmadani

Amjad Hamid

Ansi Alibava

Arif Mohamedali Vora

Ashraf Ali

Ashraf al-Masri

Ashraf el-Moursy Ragheb

Atta Elayyan

Farhaj Ahsan

Ghulam Hussain

Hafiz Musa Patel

Haji-Daoud Nabi

Hamza Mustafa

Haroon Mahmood

Husna Ahmed

Hussein al-Umari

Hussein Moustafa

Junaid Ismail

Kamel Darwish

Karam Bibi

Khaled Mustafa

Lilik Abdul Hamid

Linda Armstrong

Maheboob Khokhar

Matiullah Safi

Mohamad Moosid Mohamedhosen

Mohammed Imran Khan

Mohsin al-Harbi

Mojammel Hoq

Mounir Guirgis Soliman

Mucaad Ibrahim

Muhammad Abdus Samad

Muhammad Haziq Mohd-Tarmizi

Muse Nur Awale

Naeem Rashid

Omar Faruk

Osama Adnan Yousef Abukwaik

Ozair Kadir

Ramiz Vora

Sayyad Milne

Suhail Shahid

Syed Areeb Ahmed

Syed Jahandad Ali

Talha Naeem

Tariq Omar

Zakaria Bhuiya

Zeeshan Raza

Zekeriya Tuyan

and all those who have lost

Notes

The invocation is taken from Bhartrihari's *Śṛṅgāra Śataka*, my translation.

Notes to 'समरसि समर'

'समरसि समर', translated as 'Remember, Love?', is drawn from Kalidāsa's epic poem *Kumārasambhava*, in a lament voiced by Kāma's wife Rati. Keening over his lifeless body, she wills him to revive, reminding him how creation is destined to wilt and suffer in his absence, for all meaning in life depends on Love.

The five parts in the first section correspond to the five arrows of Kāma, viz.: 'स्तम्भन' – 'stunning/paralysing'; 'शोषण' – 'drying up/withering'; 'सम्मोहन' – 'bewildering/mesmerising'; 'उन्मादन' – 'bewitching/infatuating'; 'मारण' – 'killing/destroying'.

'ചുംബനം' translates to 'kiss' in Malayalam.

'Sleep, melancholy' draws on the mythology of two Greek gods, Hypnos (Sleep) and his brother Thanatos (Death), as described in Hesiod's *Theogony*.

'What birds plunge through is not the intimate space' is composed in the form of a cento. The following is a bibliography of works from which the lines are drawn:

Title: Rainer Maria Rilke, 'What birds plunge through is not the intimate space', translated by Stephen Mitchell, *The Selected Poetry of Rainer Maria Rilke* (Random House, 1982).

Lines 1–2: J. Allyn Rosser, 'Raven', *Misery Prefigured* (Southern Illinois University Press, 2001).

l. 3: Sappho, 'Fragment 33', translated by Anne Carson, *If Not, Winter: Fragments of Sappho* (Virago, 2003).

ll. 4–5: Mary Oliver, 'Spring', *House of Light* (Beacon Press, 1992).

ll. 6–7, 25: Kenneth Rexroth, 'When We With Sappho', *Selected Poems* (New Directions, 1984).

ll. 8–9, 16–19: Siegfried Sassoon, 'Everyone Sang', *Picture Show* (privately printed, 1919).

ll. 10–13: Richard Siken, 'The Language of the Birds', *War of the Foxes* (Copper Canyon Press, 2015).

l. 14: Hanif Abdurraqib, 'For the Dogs Who Barked at Me on the Sidewalks in Connecticut', *A Fortune For Your Disaster* (Tin House Books, 2019).

ll. 14–15: Leila Chatti, 'The Rules', *Poem-a-Day* (American Academy of Poets, 29 May 2019).

ll. 15, 21–2: Ed Roberson, 'Architektonis: Twenty for the Chicago Architecture Center', *Poetry* (June 2019).

ll. 20, 26, 27: Eavan Boland, 'We Are Always Too Late' and 'The Black Lace Fan My Mother Gave Me', *Outside History* (Carcanet Press, 1997).

ll. 23–4: Wendell Berry, 'The Peace of Wild Things', *The Selected Poems of Wendell Berry* (Counterpoint Press, 2009).

l. 28: Seamus Heaney, 'The Blackbird of Glanmore', *District and Circle* (Faber & Faber, 2006).

l. 28–30: Basavanna, '494', translated by A. K. Ramanujam, *Speaking of Śiva* (Penguin Books India, 1993).

'Self-portrait, with shyness' draws on research cited in the article 'What the Rhythm of a Maned Wolf's Heart Reveals' by Ashley Goetz, published in the Smithsonian Magazine's *Smithsonian Voices* on 8 September 2020.

'Filial, at the pyre of the body burned, three days after' references a Hindu funeral rite described in the *Grhya Sutras*, where surviving relatives of the deceased pick up the incinerated bones individually between the thumb and the fourth finger, after the body has been burned on an open pyre, on the third lunar day after death.

'A Myth of Horses' draws on varied cultural myths including the Bedouin legend of the five mares, Pegasus and the Trojan horse, the burning of Kāma, the Agni-Vadava vaktra (the fire of the mare's mouth), and the Vedic ritual of the Ashvamedha Yagna (horse sacrifice). The final stanza references a sentence from Joseph Conrad's *Heart of Darkness*, as well as a proposition from Ludwig Wittgenstein's *Philosophical Investigations*: 'If a lion could speak, we could not understand him'.

Notes to 'A is for العرب [Arabs]'

The epigraph from Ibn Rashiq is taken from *Translations of Ancient Arabian Poetry, Chiefly Pre-Islamic*, translated by Sir Charles Lyall (William & Norgate, 1885).

The children's book mentioned and quoted from on pages 51–2 is *The Velveteen Rabbit* by Margery Williams, illustrated by William Nicholson (George H. Doran, 1922).

Acknowledgements

My heartfelt gratitude to the editors of the following publications and platforms, where earlier versions or excerpts of these poems originally appeared: *Banshee, Honest Ulsterman, Irish Poetry Reading Archive, Irish University Review, Ko Aotearoa Tātou | We Are New Zealand, Poetry Ireland Review, Poetry Jukebox, Splonk and Stinging Fly.*

I am deeply indebted to the Arts Council of Ireland and The Ireland Chair of Poetry, for their invaluable support and encouragement during the completion of this work.

Thank you to everyone at Faber & Faber and Aitken Alexander, dreamcatchers all.

Swami Shubamrita, Dinesh Ghodke, John Visvader, Karen Waldron, Anne Kozak, Candice Stover, Conrad Hughes, John Cranna: For teaching me.

Kipp Quinby, Nikhit D'sa, Anmol Tikoo, Sapna Philip: Forever my frontlines.

Scott Van Note, Matteo Culotti, Seth Brandjord, Andrew Goldstein: For brotherhood.

Angela Isaac, Gina Eipe, Sneha Iype, Beena Matthew, Natasha Iype: For sisterhood.

Saeed Al Roomi, Al Marri, Alessandro Pinto, Mahendar Bhasin, Willem Malten, Jeff RP Harbour, Stephen Miller: For taking me in.

Leela Iype, Sarah Dewes, Radhika Khandpur, Shaheda Bhasin, Sheela Philip, Maya Iyer, Shobhana Iyar, Vana Menon, Anita Kapoor, Neera Dayani: For growing me up.

Cal Doyle, Jessica Traynor, Ian Maleney, Seán Hewitt, Brendan MacEvilly, Stephen Sexton, Maria McManus, Nuala O'Connor, Julie Morrissy: For gracious champions.

Christie Davis, Patrick Lannan, Margaret Kelleher, Simon O'Connor, Shelby, Gale and Kathryn Davis: For all kinds of kindness.

Summer Meline, Mícheál McCann, Marcella Prince, Eoin Rogers: For constant, generous conspirators.

Aoife Fitzpatrick, Sarah Gilmartin, David Morgan O'Connor, Aingeala Flannery: For spirited kindreds.

Declan Meade, Gráinne O'Toole, Fionnuala Cloke: For the open heart. For the open door.

Paul Perry, Gavin Corbett, Gavin McCrea: For crucibles. For flame.

Alan Gilsenan: For being, and seeing, and showing me, light.

Jeet Thayil: For the invitation into the luminous.

Maureen Kennelly: For being the mother house, when I could no longer reach mine.

Eiléan Ní Chuilleanáin: For shoring me up. For showing me how.

Sinéad Gleeson: For giving me – and taking me under your – wings.

Anne Enright: For turning my face between the finger and the moon.

Sean O'Reilly: For something almost holy. For bone.

Emma Paterson, Monica MacSwan: For your wisdom, care and affection.

Lavinia Singer, Matthew Hollis: For your vision, which sees such beauty, and so far.

My siblings, my family: For bringing me home.

O: For you, always for you.

M: Za twoja miłość, moja małpko.

Ammachi: For kisses.

Mum: For ever.

Pa: For everything. For without you, nothing.